SADDAM HUSSEIN'S

IRAQ

JAMES R. ARNOLD

TWENTY-FIRST CENTURY BOOKS   MINNEAPOLIS

Twenty-First Century Books
A division of Lerner Publishing Group, Inc.
241 First Avenue North
Minneapolis, MN 55401 U.S.A.

Website address: www.lernerbooks.com

Library of Congress Cataloging-in-Publication Data

Arnold, James R.
    Saddam Hussein's Iraq / by James R. Arnold.
      p.   cm. – (Dictatorships)
    Includes bibliographical references and index.
    ISBN 978-0-8225-8665-4 (lib. bdg. : alk. paper)
      1. Hussein, Saddam, 1937–2006. Iraq—History—1979–1991. 3. Iraq—
    History—1991–2003. I. Title.
    DS79.7.A76 2009
    956.7044—dc22   2007041//826

Manufactured in the United States of America
1 2 3 4 5 6 – DP – 14 13 12 11 10 09

CONTENTS

"THE

A CAMERAMAN PREPARES TO RECORD THE SCENE. It is July 22, 1979. Saddam Hussein has been president of Iraq for less than a week when he convenes a special conference of senior Baath Party leaders. Iraq is a one-party dictatorship run by the Baath Party, and party leaders dominate every town and village. These leaders report up the chain of command. At the top of the chain is the Revolutionary Command Council (RCC), Iraq's supreme lawmaking body. The main characteristics of the RCC and the Baath Party are secrecy and discipline. Yet Saddam has ordered that the special conference be filmed. He knows that what is about to happen will change Iraqi history, and he wants a film record so future generations will not forget.

Hundreds of Baath Party delegates from all over Iraq are seated in the conference hall. The twenty-one-member RCC is also

CRIMINALS'

SADDAM HUSSEIN SEIZED power in Iraq in 1979.

present. Saddam enters the auditorium. Flashbulbs pop. The audience rises to applaud. Dressed in a tailored suit with a neatly knotted tie and holding a large cigar in his hand, Saddam slowly approaches a pair of microphones.

Looking relaxed and self-confident, he speaks without emotion: "I wish that we could meet in happier circumstances." He goes on to deliver a dramatic announcement: a Syrian plot against the government has been discovered. Furthermore, all the plotters are present in this room! The audience gasps in astonishment. Saddam explains that loyal agents have gathered enough evidence to expose the plot. He invites an influential Iraqi politician named Muhie Abdul Hussein Mashhadi to the podium.

Eight days earlier, Mashhadi was serving as the RCC's secretary-general. He had opposed Saddam's effort to assume supreme leadership of Iraq. Saddam had ordered Mashhadi to be seized for interrogation. Agents also collected Mashhadi's family. The agents produced a list of names who they claimed were involved in a plot against the party. They gave Mashhadi a choice: he must agree to denounce the people on the list, or his interrogators would rape his wife and daughters in front of him before killing them. Then they would execute Mashhadi. Mashhadi agreed to say whatever Saddam's agents wanted.

Most of the audience members know none of this. Mashhadi appears from behind a curtain and walks to the lectern. Saddam sits down and calmly smokes his cigar. For almost two hours, Mashhadi delivers a carefully rehearsed speech. The audience listens closely as the respected Mashhadi provides details about the Syrian "plot." He adds that for the past four years he, too, has plotted against Saddam. When Mashhadi is finished, Saddam returns to the podium. Saddam says, "After the arrest of the criminals I visited them in an attempt to understand the motive for their behavior. . . . They had nothing to say to defend themselves, they just admitted their guilt." A security official reads the list of names that had been provided to Mashhadi. Armed security guards escort the alleged conspirators from the room. When one man tries to defend himself, Saddam coldly replies, "Get out, get out!"

The so-called conspirators include many men who have helped Saddam rise to power. At least one considers himself a close personal friend. Their past loyalty, however, does not matter. After the conspirators are removed from the auditorium, the remaining

ALI HASSAN AL-MAJID *(ABOVE)* **WAS A LOYAL FOLLOWER AND RELATIVE** of Iraqi dictator Saddam Hussein.

delegates vie with one another to praise Saddam. The speech of one of Saddam's cousins, Ali Hassan al-Majid, is typical: "Everything that you did in the past was good and everything that you will do in the future is good. I say this from my faith in the party and your leadership." This cousin will become known in the West years later as Chemical Ali for his use of poison gas and other chemical weapons during the fight against the Kurds of northern Iraq in 1988. He will reappear on the international stage when Iraq confronts the United States in the Iraq War of the early 2000s.

Five RCC members are among the group escorted from the hall. Saddam ends the day with a flourish by inviting the surviving RCC members to take part in the firing squads that will execute the "traitors." This will become standard practice in Saddam Hussein's Iraq. Senior leaders are compelled to participate in brutal crimes. It is all part of Saddam's psychology of terror, which keeps him in power. He calculates that by forcing such participation, these leaders forever tarnish their own reputations. They become dependent on Saddam. Their only hope to survive and prosper is to support his regime.

July 22, 1979, marks a turning point in Iraqi history. It is the day a man from humble origins assumes power to run one of history's most barbaric regimes.

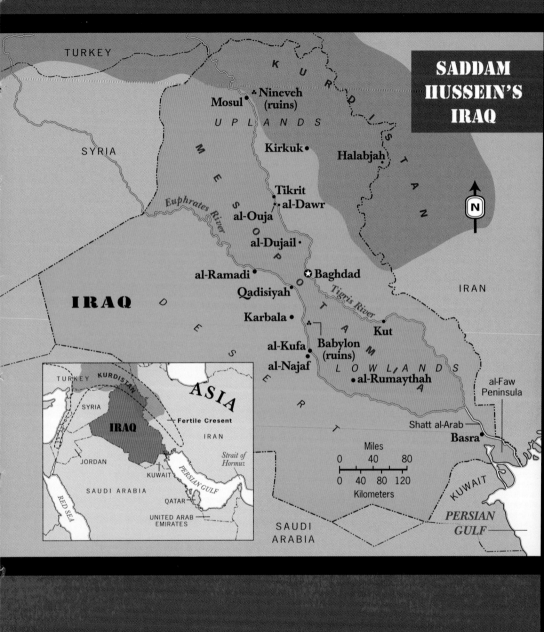

SADDAM HUSSEIN'S IRAQ

TURKEY

SYRIA

K U R D I S T A N

Mosul • ⚲ Nineveh (ruins)

U P L A N D S

Kirkuk •

Halabjah •

Tikrit
al-Dawr •
al-Ouja

al-Dujail •

IRAQ

al-Ramadi •

Qadisiyah •

Karbala •

al-Kufa •
al-Najaf

⚙ Baghdad

Euphrates River

Tigris River

M E S O P O T A M I A

D E S E R T

Babylon (ruins)

Kut •

L O W L A N D S

• al-Rumaythah

IRAN

N

al-Faw Peninsula

Shatt al-Arab

Basra •

SAUDI ARABIA

Miles

0   40   80

0   40   80   120

Kilometers

PERSIAN GULF

KUWAIT

TURKEY   KURDISTAN

SYRIA

IRAQ

ASIA

- - - Fertile Cresent

IRAN

JORDAN

KUWAIT

Strait of Hormuz

PERSIAN GULF

SAUDI ARABIA

QATAR

UNITED ARAB EMIRATES

RED SEA

IRAQ IS AN ARAB COUNTRY IN THE MIDDLE EAST, located at the north-west end of the Persian Gulf. It has a land area of 168,878 square miles (437,394 square kilometers), which means it is a little larger than California. Iraq is almost landlocked. It has only a 26-mile (42 km) coastline on the Persian Gulf. Its only useful access to the Gulf is through the Shatt al-Arab, a waterway separating Iraq and Iran. Iran borders Iraq to the east. A dispute over national boundaries and control of the Shatt al-Arab was the major cause of the Iraq–Iran War of the 1980s. Turkey lies to the north of Iraq. Syria and Jordan border Iraq on the west. Saudi Arabia and Kuwait lie to the south.

The territory of Iraq includes part of the region known as the Fertile Crescent, a semicircle-shaped region extending from the southeastern coast of the Mediterranean Sea around the Syrian Desert north of Saudi Arabia to the Persian Gulf. Great rivers

THE SHATT AL-ARAB *(ABOVE)* IS FORMED BY THE JOINING OF THE TIGRIS
River and the Euphrates River in Iraq. The Shatt al-Arab forms part of the modern
border between Iraq and Iran.

water the Fertile Crescent. Iraq's major rivers are the Tigris and
the Euphrates. People of the ancient world referred to the region
as Mesopotamia, or the Land Between the Rivers. Throughout
the Fertile Crescent are sites related to the origins of agriculture. Mesopotamia witnessed the beginning of complex societies
during the Bronze Age (about 4000 B.C.–1000 B.C.). This earned
Mesopotamia the name The Cradle of Civilization.

THE LAND

The Tigris and Euphrates rivers are Iraq's most important physical features. The headwaters of both rivers begin in the mountains of Turkey and flow in a southeasterly direction to join in lower Iraq. There they form the Shatt al-Arab, a slow-moving waterway that flows into the Persian Gulf.

Lower Iraq is a plain beginning between al-Ramadi and Baghdad and extending about 330 miles (530 km) southeastward to the Persian Gulf. Near the Persian Gulf, the area between the rivers is low-lying. Until the Iraqi government under Saddam Hussein began a massive water diversion program in the 1990s, this region featured many lesser rivers, lakes, and marshes.

Upper Iraq includes the Tigris and Euphrates River valleys to the north and northwest of Baghdad. Uplands and foothills begin to rise from the plain about 200 miles (322 km) north of Baghdad. The northeastern region along the Turkish frontier features high mountain ridges with an average summit of about 8,000 feet (2,438 meters) separated by deep river gorges. Iraq's highest elevation is an unnamed peak 12,001 feet (3,658 m) high. Iraq's western border features desert. The desert extends roughly from the Syrian and Jordanian borders southward to the border with Saudi Arabia and Kuwait.

Iraq has two climate zones. The lowlands, which comprise most of the country, has a hot, dry summer from May to October. December to March is cool and humid. The northeast, or upland, region is much cooler and wetter. Severe winters with up to three months of snow are common. However, because the upland region is small compared to the rest of Iraq, the country's climate is generally known as hot and dry.

EARLY HISTORY

From the beginning, the inhabitants of what became Iraq had to contend with floods and droughts. Iraq's ancient history turned on the struggle for control of the water supply. Two ancient kingdoms, Sumer and Akkad, fought to control the waters of the Tigris and Euphrates rivers. A great leader, King Sargon, united the realms of Sumer and Akkad around the year 2325 B.C. A period of cultural advancement followed.

A new Semitic people arrived around 2000 B.C. They established Babylon as their capital. Under the leadership of Hammurabi (1792–1750 B.C.), the first Babylonian Empire reached its height. Hammurabi was one of history's most progressive, enlightened rulers. Babylon rose as a great commercial center controlling trade between east and west. The empire of Babylonia flourished until around 1600 B.C.

The Code of Hammurabi is one of the oldest records of laws in human history. Developed during the reign of Hammurabi, the code consists of 282 case laws inscribed in stone. These laws pertain to economic matters such as prices and tariffs (taxes), family matters including marriage and divorce, civil matters such as debt, and criminal affairs including assault and theft.

Babylon's slow decline coincided with the rise of the great military kingdom of Assyria. The state of Assyria was based in the town of Nineveh near Mosul (in modern-day northern Iraq). The Assyrians used this strategic position to dominate the Tigris and Euphrates rivers. From 750 to 600 B.C., the Assyrian Empire controlled the region. The Assyrian Empire was an aggressive culture that celebrated war and conquest. The Assyrians destroyed Hammurabi's city of Babylon. Babylon rose briefly one more time under the leadership of Nebuchadnezzar (630–562 B.C.). Nebuchadnezzar was a great builder who restored Babylon to its past splendor. The archaeological remains of this Babylon still exist in Iraq.

In 539 B.C., the Persians under Cyrus, the first great captain in recorded history, conquered the region and Iraq began its long centuries under foreign rule. Around 400 B.C., Greek soldiers engaged in war against the Persians conducted the famous March of the 10,000. Among the Greeks was an Athenian officer named Xenophon who wrote a book about the campaign. The Greeks raided areas along the Euphrates, defeated a Persian army, and retreated along the Tigris. Xenophon's book contained fateful words: "Persia belongs to the man who has the courage to attack it."

In 331 B.C., a young Greek leader, Alexander the Great, took up the challenge. He swept through the region and defeated the Persians. As a result, Greek influence replaced Persian influence within what would become Iraq. Alexander died in Babylon in 323 B.C. One of Alexander's generals maintained Greek influence from a capital south of Baghdad (Iraq's modern capital) until a new Persian power, the Parthians, arose. They ruled Iraq during the height of the Roman Empire (from the first century B.C. through the second century A.D.). However, the Parthians were a nomadic people who were never able to establish unchallenged control over the region. From the east came another Persian power, the Sassanids. The Sassanids defeated the Parthians and established the Sassanid Empire in A.D. 226. For four centuries, Sassanid rule brought peace and prosperity to the war-torn region. The Sassanids repaired and extended the canal systems that controlled the sometimes deadly flooding of the Tigris and Euphrates rivers.

IRAQ AND THE RISE OF ISLAM

The prophet Muhammad (also spelled Mohammed) was born in Arabia in A.D. 570. He founded a new religion, Islam. Muhammad initially planned to use his devout warriors to expand Islam into Mesopotamia, where the Sassanid Empire held control. After Muhammad's death in 632, his successors, called caliphs, continued to expand Islam. By 636 Muslims (followers of Islam) had conquered Mesopotamia and thus controlled the entire Arabian Peninsula. Soon Arab peoples poured into the conquered lands.

Early in the history of Islam, an important religious split occurred. The disagreement concerned the method of choosing the next caliph. People who favored an elected leader came to be called Sunni Muslims. Others believed that only direct descendants of Muhammad should be caliphs. These people were called Shiite Muslims.

The caliphs became the new rulers of this ancient land. They established Baghdad as the City of the Caliphs in 762. The city prospered, becoming a commercial center. It enjoyed an advanced civilization that produced scientists, philosophers, jurists, and poets. Baghdad was renowned for its libraries. At a time when Europe was declining in the Early Middle Ages (about 476–1000), Baghdad was already an advanced intellectual center. During the Early Middle Ages, Europe produced little written history and failed to preserve many documents that had been written in earlier Roman and Greek times. In contrast, scholars in Baghdad were copying and translating documents and books from all over the known world. Many classical European works survived into modern times because of this effort. One example is Euclid's *Elements of Geometry*.

In this golden age, scholars came to Baghdad from throughout the world. It was a place where Arab, Persian, and Greek cultures flourished simultaneously. The famous stories of *The Thousand and One Nights* relate the history of the greatest of the caliphs. At the same time, violent warfare characterized the region. Some of the most bitter fighting was among the caliphs themselves. Internal disputes split the caliphate (an area ruled by caliphs), but it was an external force that eventually overthrew their control of Mesopotamia.

THIS IS A PAGE FROM EUCLID'S *Elements of Geometry* **from the twelfth century and translated into Arabic. Works such as this were preserved through the efforts of scholars in Baghdad.**

Many ancient cities still have impressive archaeological remains. Athens, Greece, preserves numerous ancient Greek sites. Rome, Italy, has the Forum and the Coliseum. Cairo, Egypt, has the pyramids and other ancient and medieval sites. In contrast, most of medieval Baghdad no longer exists. In 2003, the last year of Saddam Hussein's rule, the largest, most impressive structures were the countless sculptures, mosques (Islamic places of worship), and palaces glorifying Saddam.

In the middle of the thirteenth century, Asian leader Hulagu Khan led his Mongol and Tatar warriors westward. They swept through Mesopotamia and wiped out the Arab caliphs. Hulagu's men slaughtered people and animals and left burning villages and towns in their wake. In 1258 they sacked Baghdad, piling the skulls of their victims outside the city's gates. So few people remained that the canals and irrigation systems could not be maintained. As a result, the once-rich land became desolate and barren.

The Ottoman Empire (based in what became modern Turkey) was the next foreign power to control Mesopotamia. The Ottomans came south from Turkey to establish rule in 1534. The area encompassing modern Iraq remained under Turkish control until World

War I (1914–1918). The Turks established three provinces based on the major trading cities of Mosul in the north, Baghdad in the center, and Basra in the south. During this period, the Ottoman Empire was mainly interested in Iraq as a source of tribute (excessive taxes imposed by powerful leaders). Urban Sunnis (followers of a branch of Islam) held important positions under the Ottomans and gradually came to dominate Iraqi politics. Outside of the main cities and towns, the Ottomans held little influence. Consequently, rural areas fell under the control of various tribal leaders. Here the powerful prospered by taking what they wanted from the less powerful. During almost four hundred years of Turkish control, Iraq remained backward and poor.

OIL AND FOREIGN CONTROL

In 1908 oil was discovered in the Middle East. The first discovery came at Masjid Suleiman in Iran. The outbreak of World War I shortly thereafter in 1914 pitted the Allies, led by Great Britain and France, against the Central powers, which included Germany, Austria, and the Ottoman Empire. Great Britain tried to wrest control of Mesopotamia, Palestine, and Syria from the Turks. In Mesopotamia the British were particularly interested in controlling oil resources. An Anglo-Indian force (India was part of the British Empire at this time) captured the Iraqi port of Basra in 1914. The following year, a British column advanced inland to capture the city of Kut. In March 1917, the British and their Arab allies captured Baghdad. The Turks continued to hold out in the north around the city of Mosul until the war ended.

Even before the war ended, Great Britain and France were deep in negotiations about who should control the region's oil

BRITISH SOLDIERS ENTERED MESOPOTAMIA DURING WORLD WAR I. ALONG with Indian soldiers, they fought against what was then the Ottoman Empire.

wealth after the expected downfall of the Ottoman Empire. As far back as 1916, Great Britain and France had decided to divide the lands they captured from the Turks. A British lieutenant colonel, Sir Mark Sykes, and a French diplomat, François George-Picot, signed a secret agreement on May 16, 1916. The Sykes-Picot Agreement defined areas of influence after the war. The agreement took little notice of the region's religious, tribal, and ethnic boundaries. It was created instead for the advantage of Great Britain and France. Some historians argue that the agreement was a turning point in Western–Arab relations. At this time, many Arabs of the Middle East wanted greater self-rule. The influential Brit T. E. Lawrence—a writer, soldier, and archaeologist known as Lawrence of Arabia—had promised these Arab nationalists that they would obtain an Arab national homeland in exchange for siding with the British during the war against the Ottoman Empire. The Sykes-Picot Agreement invalidated this promise, and Arab nationalists felt betrayed.

According to the Sykes-Picot Agreement, France was to keep Mosul while Great Britain retained the rest of Mesopotamia. Mosul was particularly valuable because it was the first place oil was discovered in Iraq.

A period of intrigue and scheming followed. Within the British government, disagreement arose over how to rule Mesopotamia. Meanwhile, Arab nationalists sought self-rule and began voicing their displeasure with British rule. In 1919 British administrators proposed joining the three old Turkish provinces—namely Mosul,

DRILLING TOWERS STARTED TO APPEAR IN IRAQ AFTER THE DISCOVERY of oil in 1908. After World War I, France and Great Britain divided the conquered territory according to its oil wealth.

Baghdad, and Basra—into a single new country. Europeans who knew the region judged that this plan was a recipe for disaster. The three provinces contained three distinct peoples. The Kurds dominated the north around Mosul. Sunni Muslims dominated the center around Baghdad. Shiite Muslims dominated the south around Basra. All three groups wanted full independence. None of the three trusted one another, nor did they support the idea of uniting to form a new country. One of the few beliefs shared among the groups was that the British had betrayed their desire for self-rule.

A BRITISH MANDATE

In April 1920, at San Remo, Italy, the Allied victors of World War I divided the lands they had conquered. Iraq became a Class A British mandate. This mandate was supposed to be a temporary status leading to independence. In the view of Arab nationalists, the San Remo agreement provided proof that Great Britain had betrayed them. As one Arab nationalist explained to a British writer, "Since you took Baghdad, you have been talking about an Arab government, but three years or more have elapsed and nothing has materialised."

During May 1920, a series of mass meetings took place in Baghdad to denounce the mandate. Sunnis and Shiites worked together to promote Iraqi independence. The British continued to insist on limitations to self-rule. On July 2, 1920, a revolt began in al-Rumaythah, on the lower Euphrates. The overt cause was high taxes. The revolt spread quickly and became a rebellion against the British presence in Iraq. At the height of the revolt during the summer and early autumn, about 130,000 fighters opposed the British. An estimated 6,000 Iraqis and 500 British and Indian soldiers died in the fighting. The British suppressed the rebels and reestablished control by February 1921.

The rebellion forced the British government to consider how it could maintain order in such a turbulent region. The British solution was to use its mandate from the League of Nations (an international peacekeeping body) to install a handpicked candidate as king. King Faisal was crowned in Baghdad on August 23, 1921. He proved a weak leader, which was fine with the British, who were much more interested in exploiting the Mosul oil fields than in promoting Iraqi nationalism.

As time passed, overt British control diminished although British advisers continued to work alongside Iraqi officials who took the advisers' place. The British High Commissioner for Iraq, Sir Percy Cox, described the goal of British policy: "The Iraqi Government must be allowed to make mistakes and learn by them during this probationary [mandate] period, provided that such mistakes are not of a nature to lead to disaster and that British troops and officers are not forced to be instruments of misgovernment." The British mandate ended in September 1932. On October 3, 1932, Iraq officially became an independent nation. King Faisal died on September 8, 1933. Before his death, the king wrote a confidential memo. The memo predicted a grim future where there would be repeated rebellions against the government.

King Faisal's twenty-one-year-old son, Ghazi, became king. The lack of established political parties and recognized legal methods to make change led to political and social turmoil. Politicians who sought change had few choices. They could try to embarrass the government and thus cause its downfall. They could incite tribal uprisings that would cause the government to fail. These two methods caused the fall of four governments between 1932 and 1934. Instability led to more instability. It also gave rise to a third way to create change: military action. And, as history throughout the world showed, once a military group took over the government, it was difficult for civilian rule to return.

COUPS AND WORLD WAR II

Iraq's first military coup occurred in 1936. A group of young Socialists obtained the backing of General Bakr Sidqi. Bakr, in turn, obtained the support of the army and overthrew the government. Bakr promised to enact widespread social reform. He invited left-wing (Socialist) politicians to participate in the government. His Socialist inclinations annoyed old-line military men, as well as opposition politicians. On August 11, 1937, a group of military officers assassinated Bakr. Six more coups quickly followed. Through them the army dominated political decision making in Iraq.

Meanwhile, a rising Iraqi middle class objected to continuing British domination and a growing nationalist movement spread through the Iraqi military. World War II (1939–1945) provided a new opportunity for these groups to assert themselves. By 1941 Nazi Germany had conquered most of Europe. Great Britain alone resisted Germany. Iraqi nationalists sensed that Britain was weak and vulnerable.

A group of Iraqi nationalists, led by a pro-Nazi prime minister named Rashid Ali, plotted to eliminate lingering British influence in Iraq. Four army colonels, known as the Golden Square, led an attack against a British air base in Iraq. The effort failed dismally. Rashid Ali and some of his henchmen fled the country. The British captured and hanged the four colonels. The British rounded up and imprisoned lesser rebel leaders, including Khairallah Tulfah, the beloved uncle of young Saddam Hussein.

During World War II, the United States and its ally Russia issued statements favoring democratic freedoms for people living under colonial rule. (The United States joined the war in 1941 after the Japanese attacked the U.S. naval base at Pearl Harbor, Hawaii.) Many Iraqi people took heart from these statements and became active in national politics. During the war, the Iraqi people lived under press censorship and many consumer goods were rationed to help support the British war effort. They expected the situation to improve when peace came, but it did not.

At this time, Amir Abd al-Ilah ruled Iraq. He served as regent (ruler) for his nephew, the boy king Faisal II. During the war, al-Ilah's government paid little attention to the wishes of the Iraqi people. The regent attributed public disaffection to the lack of a true parliamentary (lawmaking) system. In 1945 he called for the formation of political parties, full political freedom, and social and economic reform. Iraqis greeted this news enthusiastically. But those already in power blocked meaningful reform. When a new government formed in January 1946 in response to the regent's wishes, it lasted only a few months before politicians representing entrenched interests overthrew it.

A succession of governments came and went until 1958. A small group of young military officers began plotting revolution. Calling themselves the Free Officers, they formed revolutionary cells and worked in secret. Although the group was few in number, many people sympathized with their nationalist goals. On July 14, 1958, the Free Officers overthrew the Iraqi government. They proclaimed the end of the monarchy and the beginning of a new republic (state run by elected representatives).

The coup was very popular within Iraq. The poor and unemployed were particularly hopeful that better days lay ahead. Almost everyone welcomed the arrival of a government that would free them from foreign influence while putting the nation's oil wealth to work for the benefit of Iraqis.

An army officer, General Abdul Karim Qasim, the leader of the Free Officers, became head of the government. His government declared that Iraq was part of a greater Arab nation and that within Iraq, Arabs and Kurds would be equals. Islam was to be the

LEFT: **KING FAISAL II** *(CENTER)* **OF IRAQ GREETS A BRITISH LORD IN 1956. HIS** regent, Amir Abd al-Ilah, watches *(left)*. *Right:* General Abdul Karim Qasim became head of the government after a coup removed Faisal II from power.

state religion. A Sovereignty Council and the cabinet were to hold all executive and legislative powers. But in fact, Qasim held the most power and his support came not from the people but from the army.

PAN-ARABISM AND THE RISE OF THE BAATH PARTY

Internal conflicts among the Free Officers soon arose. Moreover, the issue of pan-Arabism—a philosophy in which Arab nations join together to create a single Arab entity—divided Iraq. Iraq's Arab nationalists supported pan-Arabism. Iraqi Communists and the Kurds, who were not Arab, opposed pan-Arabism. This conflict eventually undermined Qasim's government.

Qasim's rule lasted until February 1963. By the end of his rule, he had become unpopular within Iraq. Among foreign governments, only the Soviet Union had supported Qasim's rule. Lacking internal or foreign support, the government was ripe for a fall. A military faction (group) supported by an Arab nationalist party started a rebellion on February 8, 1963. Qasim's government collapsed, and Qasim was executed. The military did not want to run the government directly. So it handed over control of the government to its nationalist party ally, the Iraqi branch of the pan-Arab Socialist Baath Party.

The Baath Party had initially supported Qasim. However, when Qasim turned away from the notion of union with other Arab states, the Baath Party leaders—who supported pan-Arabism partly in an effort to end Western colonialism in the region—felt betrayed.

Consequently, they had resolved to overthrow Qasim and enthusiastically supported the 1963 rebellion. Baath leaders invited Abdul Salam Arif to become president. A Baathist military officer, Colonel Ahmad Hassan al-Bakr, became prime minister. Military and civilian leaders joined a National Council for Revolutionary Command and took over legislative and executive powers. Henceforth, Iraq's history became closely linked to the history of the Baath Party, as well as to one of its rising stars—Saddam Hussein.

AHMAD HASSAN AL-BAKR *(ABOVE)* became prime minister of Iraq under Abdul Salam Arif in 1963. This photo was taken in 1976.

THE
DICTATOR'S

SADDAM HUSSEIN WAS BORN IN THE 1930S in the village of al-Ouja (Awja) in north central Iraq. The village's name means "the turning," so named because it was on a sharp bend in the Tigris River, about 5 miles (8 km) from the town of Tikrit. Historically, al-Ouja was known as a haven for bandits who preyed on traders and merchants using the nearby river. In the twentieth century, the region remained one of the poorest in the country. Most villagers worked as domestic servants in Tikrit or as farm laborers on nearby estates. At the time of Saddam's birth, al-Ouja consisted of mud huts and shabby houses. There were no paved roads, running water, or electricity.

The details of Saddam's birth are unknown. Even the exact birth date is disputed, although April 28, 1937, is his official birthday. Some say that he was born in 1935. Others claim 1939. Regardless

RISE TO POWER

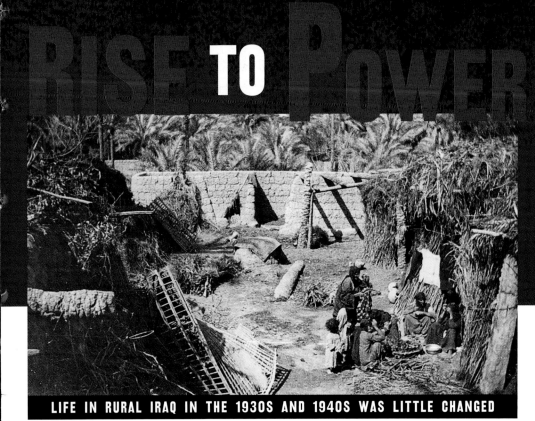

LIFE IN RURAL IRAQ IN THE 1930S AND 1940S WAS LITTLE CHANGED from life in earlier centuries.

of the year, Saddam was born into a poor family. His father probably died several months before his birth.

A TROUBLED YOUTH

Saddam's mother remarried when Saddam was about three years old. Her second marriage led to a decline in the family's local status.

Villagers recalled, "The Majids [her first husband's family] had a bad reputation, but the Ibrahims [her second husband's family] were even worse." Saddam's stepfather is said to have abused him. He also prevented Saddam from attending school and instead forced the youngster into a life of crime to help support the family. Because of his lowly social status, Saddam was ridiculed by village children and bullied by villagers. Saddam's unhappy early years resulted in his becoming self-reliant and callous. He learned to trust no one outside of his immediate family.

A tradition in the region where Saddam was born was to raise boys to become tough. Aunts or uncles often raised the male children so the boys would escape from tender parental influence. Saddam's most important early influence was his maternal uncle, Khairallah Tulfah. Khairallah inspired the young Saddam with strong nationalistic feelings and taught him a deep dislike of the Iraqi royal family and their foreign supporters, namely Great Britain.

Khairallah was an officer serving in the Iraqi army. He was an ardent Arab nationalist, as well as an enthusiastic admirer of Nazi Germany. A pamphlet Khairallah wrote—*Three Whom God Should Not Have Created: Persians, Jews, Flies*—reflected his extreme beliefs. Khairallah's pro-Nazi views resulted in his imprisonment by British authorities in 1941. He remained in prison for five years. One of young Saddam's happiest days came when his uncle was released from prison. Saddam then lived with Khairallah in Tikrit. His uncle first encouraged him to complete grade school in Tikrit. Saddam hoped to be accepted into the Baghdad Military Academy, but he was unable to pass the entrance examination. Later in life, as dictator, he controlled all aspects of the Iraqi military.

After completing his primary education in 1955, Saddam moved to Baghdad with his uncle to attend high school. As a poor young man from a backward rural area entering a vibrant urban setting, this was a turning point in his life. While attending school, Saddam worked at various part-time jobs to earn extra money. He sold cigarettes, was a driver's assistant, and worked in a coffeehouse. In the 1950s, Baghdad was enjoying newfound prosperity stemming from the nation's oil wealth. The city was the center of Iraqi political activity. At this time, Arab nationalism was surging. At the same time, Great Britain was withdrawing from its colonial empire. This withdrawal encouraged Iraqi nationalists to think that they, too, could discard the British-installed government that ruled Iraq.

Khairallah, his family, and Saddam lived in a rough area on the western outskirts of Baghdad. It was a mixed neighborhood of Sunnis and Shiites. The two factions often fought with each other. Khairallah worked as a schoolteacher, using his position to promote his political views. He hosted political meetings in his home. These meetings brought Saddam into contact with one of Khairallah's cousins, a Tikriti army officer named Ahmad Hassan al-Bakr.

BAATH PARTY BEGINNINGS

Bakr was a leader of a newly formed political party called the Baath Party. (*Baath* means "resurrection" or "renaissance.") Three French-educated Syrian intellectuals had founded the Arab Baath Socialist Party in the early 1940s. It was a revolutionary party with a doctrine that combined religious language with a strong pan-Arab national-ism. Pan-Arab nationalism promotes the belief that all Arabs should unite to form a single Arab nation. An early party slogan was "One Arab nation with an eternal message." The Baath Party wanted to ignore the arbitrary territorial boundaries imposed by Western entities, especially Great Britain. The Baath Party also wanted a fairer distribution of the region's oil wealth. In sum the Baath Party was a revolutionary party dedicated to imposing its vision on the region. It was also violently opposed to Russian-backed Communism. Saddam impressed Bakr. Bakr became his mentor and introduced him to other Baath Party supporters.

The Baath Party motto is "Unity, Freedom, Socialism." Unity means Arab unity. Freedom emphasizes freedom from foreign control and interference. Socialism refers to Arab-style Socialism rather than to Marxism (Arab Socialism has a strong religious component while Marxism is atheist).

WOULD-BE ASSASSIN

While Khairallah became involved in Iraqi politics, Saddam became a leader of a gang of street thugs. According to custom, peasant youngsters from Tikrit had three small dots tattooed on their wrist. Whereas some boys later removed these tattoos to conceal their humble background, Saddam proudly kept his. His strong ties to Tikrit would always be a major part of his personal and political life.

In his late teens, he was very tall and muscular by Iraqi standards. On the streets, Saddam's physical size gave him power and authority. Because of his upbringing and lack of good education, Saddam spoke with a peasant accent. His grammar was poor. He used slang expressions that originated in Tikrit. More sophisticated people made fun of his peasant ways. Over time they would learn that this was a grave mistake.

Meanwhile, the boy king Faisal II had come of age and become Iraq's ruler. Three main opposition parties, the National Democratic Party, the Iraqi Communist Party, and the small but influential Baath Party sought the end of the monarchy. They cooperated to support the Free Officers. On July 14, 1958, this secret, revolutionary movement within the military overthrew the government and killed the king. Saddam's role in this event is unknown. Army general Abdul Karim Qasim, the leader of the Free Officers, became head of the government.

By late 1958, Saddam's uncle Khairallah became director of education in Baghdad. A Communist Party member named Hajj Sadoun al-Tikriti did not like Khairallah. Hajj Sadoun provided information to the government, which led authorities to fire Khairallah. This enraged Khairallah, who ordered Saddam to exact revenge. The twenty-one-year-old Saddam, in turn, shot and killed Hajj Sadoun. Saddam and his uncle were arrested and placed in prison for six months. There was not enough evidence to bring them to trial, however, so they were set free. The effect of this incident was a rise in Saddam's status within the Baath Party. In their view, Saddam was a young, tough, and dedicated member.

Saddam emerged from jail to work as a bus conductor. But his real interest was the Iraqi nationalist movement, and he became increasingly involved in Baath Party politics. At this time, the party had fewer than one thousand members. General Qasim's government had begun purging (removing based on undesirability) Baathists and other nationalists. This action infuriated the Baath Party. The party saw Saddam as a useful tool to help overthrow General Qasim's government. As one party member recalled, the

SADDAM THE ASSASSIN: THE MYTH AND THE REALITY

The 1959 assassination attempt on General Qasim occurred when Saddam drew his gun and opened fire at Qasim's passing vehicle. A confused firefight ensued during which Qasim's chauffeur and one of the assassins were killed and both Qasim and Saddam were wounded. Probably Saddam was hit accidentally by one of the assassins. His wound was not serious. A sympathetic doctor tended to it, and then Saddam fled Baghdad. He first returned to his home village of al-Ouja and then left the country to live in exile.

What in reality had been a botched assassination attempt became an important part of Saddam's legend. Saddam devised an epic story accounting for these events. After he became dictator, he spread this version through a novel written by a supporter. Titled *The Long Days*, the novel depicts a heroic man of the people who uses his cunning and courage for the greater benefit of Iraq. In one passage, the novel dramatically states, "Only God knows who gave him his superhuman strength in those critical hours."

party "needed to bring someone like Saddam in off the streets to do the dirty work for them." Saddam joined a group assigned the task of assassinating Qasim. The attempt came on October 7, 1959. Five marksmen, including Saddam, tried to shoot Qasim, but the attempt failed. The reason they failed remains clouded in controversy. Most likely, the assassins failed due to their inexperience. Saddam himself probably opened fire too soon. What is certain is that the assassins had to flee for their lives.

Later, the novel formed the basis for a biographical film produced by Iraq's Ministry of Information. The film, also titled *The Long Days*, appeared frequently on Iraqi television during the 1980s. The film portrays Saddam as a heroic figure who does not flinch when a comrade removes a bullet from his leg using a pair of scissors. Then, because he can barely walk, Saddam buys a horse and rides to Tikrit. He spends the night with a Bedouin tribesman and then travels on toward Syria. His only food is bread and dates until he happens upon a wedding party. They have slaughtered a sheep, and Saddam shares a hearty meal with them. He continues on horseback until intercepted by two carloads of customs officials. He cannot outrun the officials, so he courageously confronts them and manages to talk his way out of trouble. At another point, he places his knife in his mouth and swims across the Tigris River to safety.

The film had little basis in truth. Yet it succeeded in persuading many viewers that Saddam was a courageous, intrepid warrior who suffered greatly in a noble effort to change the government. Within Iraq the myth of Saddam replaced the truth.

LIFE IN EXILE

Saddam lived in exile for three and a half years, first in Syria and then in Egypt. At this time, Damascus, Syria, was the spiritual home of Baathism. Cairo, Egypt, was the center of Arab nationalism. Saddam's experiences in these two cities greatly influenced him. One of the founding fathers of the Baath Party was a Syrian named Michel Aflaq. Aflaq took a personal interest in Saddam. Aflaq made Saddam a full party member, which was a great honor.

THIS PORTRAIT OF SADDAM WAS taken in the early 1960s.

In 1960 Saddam enrolled in a Cairo high school. An Egyptian official described Saddam at this time: "He was quiet, disciplined, and didn't ask for extra funds like the other exiles. He didn't have much interest in alcohol or girls." Saddam completed high school and enrolled in the University of Cairo in 1961, where he studied law. He did not complete his law studies. However, several years later, after he returned to Iraq, Saddam showed up to take the annual law exam at Baghdad University. He wore a full military uniform. He placed his revolver on his desk as he sat down. This was enough to intimidate the instructor, who awarded Saddam a law degree.

In early 1963, Saddam returned to Iraq. He was a changed man. An acquaintance wrote: "When he fled Baghdad, he had not even finished high school. He was a thuggish kid who was good with his fists. But the Saddam who returned from Cairo was better educated and more adult." While still in Cairo, Saddam became engaged to his cousin Sajida, the daughter of his beloved uncle Khairallah. By marrying his cousin, Saddam was following Iraqi peasant tradition. The two formally married in 1963. Later, Saddam told an interviewer that he and Sajida were betrothed to each other when she was a child. He said, "As I grew older the feelings of love increased, naturally, but I couldn't tell her of my feelings towards her even though we were one family."

SADDAM MARRIED HIS COUSIN
Sajida *(above)* in 1963.

During the time of Saddam's exile, the Baath Party had prospered. Saddam returned to Iraq after Qasim was overthrown by a group of military officers led by Saddam's former mentor, General Ahmad Hassan al-Bakr. The U.S. Central Intelligence Agency (CIA) supported this coup because Bakr was strongly anti-Communist, as was the United States. Bakr became prime minister under the new president, Abdul Salam Arif. Bakr rewarded men from his native Tikrit by giving them important positions in the government. Bakr had befriended both Saddam and his uncle Khairallah back in 1959. Bakr tried to help Saddam. However, the established Iraqi Baathist Party did not accept the validity of Saddam's membership, which had been given to him while in exile. Consequently, Bakr could give Saddam only a minor post at the Central Farmer's Office.

In that position, Saddam worked hard to track down Communists and Communist sympathizers. He was so zealous that the Baath Party appointed him to its intelligence committee. This committee was in charge of interrogations, which often involved torture. Probably at this time, Saddam began to take part in torturing suspected Communists.

In 1964, within nine months of the new government seizing power, President Arif tried to take full control. He may have been reacting to fears of a Baathist plot to overthrow him. He put Bakr under house arrest and ordered Saddam arrested. Saddam went into hiding, but authorities captured him. Saddam spent the next two years in jail. In 1966 President Arif died in a helicopter crash. His brother succeeded him. The Baath Party sensed another opportunity and sent word to Saddam to try to escape from prison. On July 23, 1966, Saddam and a fellow prisoner were being taken to court for their trial. Saddam convinced his guards to stop for lunch at a restaurant. During the meal, he went to the restroom and then out a back door to a waiting car driven by one of his cousins. He went into hiding again.

REVOLUTION

The Baath Party staged a revolution on July 17, 1968, and seized power. It was the fourth coup in ten years. The army supported the coup. Saddam was in military uniform and riding a tank when a military unit broke into the Presidential Palace to overthrow the president. Bakr took office. His job titles included president, commander in chief, chairman of the ruling Regional Command Council, and secretary-general of the Baath Party. Saddam Hussein was his aide and deputy.

Henceforth, the Baath Party worked to create a one-party dictatorship. Membership in the Baath Party was necessary for any Iraqi to advance his career. The party, in turn, observed a strict hierarchy. At the base was the neighborhood unit. Each unit reported up the chain of command to the division, the section, and finally the branch. Each of Iraq's eighteen provinces had one branch, and the capital at Baghdad had three branches. At the top was the state's highest executive and legislative body, the Regional Command Council. The Baath Party enacted a new constitution in 1970 that placed the ruling members of the Regional Command Council in the Revolutionary Command Council (RCC).

The RCC made the laws and issued decrees. It alone could mobilize the army, approve a state budget, make treaties, and begin and end wars. Saddam was the RCC's vice president. Whereas all the other top officials had worked their way up the party hierarchy, Saddam achieved his place because of his connection with Bakr. The main characteristics of the RCC and the Baath Party were secrecy and discipline. These characteristics fit Saddam's style.

In 1968 the entire Baath Party in Iraq had an estimated membership of only several thousand. Its leadership came from a small number of Sunni families living around Tikrit. This was a very narrow political base. Consequently, Saddam set out to ensure party control by ruthlessly squashing all potential opposition.

As Bakr's power increased, so did Saddam's. Saddam worked at building up the Baathist internal security structure. This structure would eventually provide him with the means to become a dictator. Saddam's goal was to build an organization that could deal with external enemies and internal dissidents. Ordinary Iraqis were taught to fear and respect the party. One method to accomplish this was the show trial (a trial, usually of political opponents, in which the verdict is rigged and a public confession is often extracted).

A stunning example came in 1969. Iraq shared with the rest of the Arab world a hatred of Israel and its Jewish citizens. This hatred became more intense after Israel's victory over its Arab neighbors in the Six Day War of June 1967. On December 14, 1968, the Iraqi government announced that it had arrested members of an Israeli spy network. Iraqi television and radio featured confessions from two supposed spies. The government accused two Iraqi Jews of being the leaders of the spy network. Bakr personally addressed anti-Israel demonstrations in Iraq and helped create an atmosphere of mass hysteria. Bakr would call out to the crowd, "What do you want?" The crowd would reply, "Death to the spies, execution of the spies, all the spies, without delay!"

REVOLUTIONARY COURT

Saddam set up a special Revolutionary Court to try seventeen alleged plotters. Thirteen of the seventeen were Jews. As a show trial, the verdict was never in doubt. Even the so-called defense attorney asked the court to punish the "traitors." Defendants were tortured and their families and friends threatened. Then cameras recorded the scene for public viewing as victim after victim "confessed" his crimes. The executions would take place in Baghdad's Liberation Square on January 27, 1969. Government radio invited the public "to come and enjoy the feast." A government minister addressed the assembled crowd with the promise that it was only the beginning: "The great and immortal squares of Iraq shall be filled up with the corpses of traitors and spies!"

SADDAM *(RIGHT AT MICROPHONE)* **SPEAKS TO A CROWD ON JANUARY 27, 1969,** after the execution of fourteen Iraqis charged with spying for Israel.

The Baath Party kept its promise. Soon public trials and executions were commonplace. People began to refer to Liberation Square, where most executions took place, as the Square of the Hanged. Saddam's goal was to use the Revolutionary Court to eliminate anyone hostile to the Bakr regime and to kill potential rivals.

Because the Baath Party was anti-Communist, Western powers including the United States who shared this stance were inclined to support it. In their view, an Iraq dominated by Baathists was better than an Iraq controlled by Communists. With this in mind, the British ambassador to Iraq met with Saddam in December 1969. At this time, Saddam was not well known in the West. The ambassador provided his assessment: "I should judge him, young as he is, to be a formidable, single-minded and hard-headed member of the Ba'athist hierarchy, but one with whom . . . it would be possible to do business."

SOPHISTICATED SADDAM

During the five years following the revolution of the late 1960s, Saddam rose to become the second most powerful man in Iraq. He had acquired a more polished demeanor and public relations skills. His rough, tough peasant demeanor was gone. He had developed a liking for luxury and wore elegant tailored suits, imported silk ties, and a platinum diamond-studded watch with diamond cuff links. He gave interviews to foreign journalists at Baghdad's finest restaurants, where he smoked expensive Cuban cigars and drank imported whiskey. A journalist noted that while Baathist propaganda described Saddam as a committed revolutionary, in reality he was living a luxurious life in a palace on the banks of the Tigris River.

While enjoying a rich life, Saddam kept his focus on his next goal: strengthening his position so he would replace President Bakr. By 1974 Bakr's health had declined substantially. This made it easier for Saddam to promote himself to the rank of general in January 1976. He installed supporters, almost all of whom were fellow Tikritis, throughout the government. In October 1977, Bakr appointed Colonel Adnan Khairallah as minister of defense. Conveniently for Saddam, Khairallah was his cousin and brother-in-law. This appointment was another example of how family and tribal ties connected Saddam to the reins of government.

The Baath Party extended its influence throughout Iraq. The party intruded into all parts of Iraqi society. Non-Baathist government workers were dismissed from their jobs. Every town and village became dominated by Baath Party leaders. These leaders reported up the chain of command. With each passing month, Saddam sat more firmly at the head of this chain. The Baath Party also installed "morale officers" and party commissioners whose job was to keep watch over other party members. Early in 1976, the party doubled the size of the People's Militia. This militia was the party's own military force and served as a counterweight to the regular armed forces.

Always lurking in the background was the intelligence service, which Saddam also controlled. His security forces conducted nighttime raids on private homes to arrest people. Often their victims were never seen again. Iraq became "a place where men vanished, and their friends were too frightened to inquire what had happened to them; people arrested on trivial charges 'committed suicide' in prison; former officials were mysteriously assassinated; politicians disappeared." From time to time, rumors emerged that Saddam personally conducted torture sessions. Whether true or not, such rumors helped create a climate of fear.

CHAPTER 5

PRESIDENT

THE BAATH PARTY HAD ALWAYS SUPPORTED pan-Arabism. This ideal had never caught on in most of the Arab world, however. The Baath Party had managed to build substantial support only in Iraq and Syria. In the fall of 1978, Bakr proposed merging with Syria to fight Israel as a bold political ploy in an attempt to limit Saddam's power.

On October 1, 1978, Bakr took the first step by announcing that he was ready to send Iraqi troops to reinforce Syria. Bakr believed that the Baath Party would support him in this effort. However, the head of the Syrian government, Hafiz al-Asad, doubted Bakr had the power and ability to accomplish a merger of the two nations. Asad correctly judged that Saddam actually held most of the power in Iraq. Consequently, Asad did not support Bakr's efforts at unification.

By 1979 Saddam judged the situation ripe to become president of Iraq. He had installed spies and informers throughout the military and the government. His security services monitored all phone and postal communications. He persuaded Bakr to appear on national television on July 16, 1979, to announce that Saddam would replace him. The details of this transfer of power remain shrouded in secrecy. What is certain is that during a special closed session of the RCC five days earlier, the decision was made to replace Bakr. All Bakr's powers and most of his titles were transferred to Saddam.

Then Saddam convened a special conference of senior Baath Party leaders. He announced the existence of a Syrian plot to overthrow him and conducted a broad purge of the top Baathist command. One-third of the RCC members were executed. Saddam's agents oversaw the removal of anyone suspected of opposing him within the Baath Party, army, militia, trade unions, student groups, and professional associations. To help accomplish this, Iraqi television screens flashed a phone number that was supposedly Saddam's personal number. People were encouraged to call this number to provide the names of "enemies of the revolution."

This event marked a turning point in Iraqi history. The Baath Party had promoted the ideal of collective leadership. But now power was no longer shared among Baathist officials. Instead, Saddam Hussein was in charge of everything. He was called the Leader. Saddam's strategy to maintain control consisted of four elements: extreme violence to shape society; use of state resources— jobs, patronage, and economic incentives—to buy loyalty; use of oil wealth to finance select projects; and exploitation of ethnic and communal differences to divide peoples and rule them.

Because the military possessed the strength to challenge him, Saddam immediately set out to win it over. He raised salaries, gave officers better housing and access to superior consumer goods, and vastly increased spending on the military. Officers who actively supported Saddam and the Baath Party found that, among their many advantages, their sons were being accepted by Iraq's best military schools.

For the civilian population, Saddam used the nation's oil wealth to create a comprehensive welfare state (a system in which the government takes primary responsibility for the individual and social well-being of its citizens). The government offered such services as free health care, housing subsidies, retirement pensions, and free reading classes to improve literacy rates. At the same time, Saddam began a series of major construction projects to modernize Iraq's infrastructure (for example, roads, highways, bridges, and railroads). The Iraqi people, in turn, accepted Saddam for several reasons. First, they lived in a state of constant fear. Second, they wanted a ruler who would bring stability after such a long period of frequent changes in government. Third, citizens took pride in seeing their country transformed into a modern nation.

THE IRAN–IRAQ WAR

During the time Saddam rose to leadership of Iraq, important political changes also occurred in neighboring Iran. The Iranian government collapsed following widespread uprisings in 1978 and 1979. A nationwide referendum in March 1979 resulted in a massive vote favoring the establishment of an Islamic republic in Iran. Ayatollah Ruhollah Khomeini became the supreme leader.

AYATOLLAH RUHOLLAH KHOMEINI *(CENTER)* **SPEAKS TO AN AUDIENCE AT THE** airport in Tehran after returning to Iran in 1979. A month after his return, he was elected the supreme leader of Iran.

Khomeini's revolutionary government based its policies on Islamic fundamentalism (strict adherence to ancient Islamic law). This alarmed Saddam, who worried that Khomeini's brand of religion would spread to Iraq's majority Shiite population, which might then threaten to depose Saddam. Indeed, Khomeini did not hide his desire to export the Islamic revolution to Iraq. Khomeini provided both moral and material support for dissident Iraqi groups. For example, he sheltered outlawed Iraqi Shiite groups who were trying to overthrow Saddam.

As tensions between Iran and Iraq mounted, Saddam began planning for war with Iran. Saddam judged that a quick military success against Iran would make Iraq the region's dominant power. As Iraq's leader, he would assume the mantle of Arab nationalism. His immediate goal was to secure the eastern bank of the Shatt al-Arab, the waterway separating Iraq from Iran. Control of both banks of this strategic waterway would give Iraq safe passage for oil exports. In addition, Saddam hoped to capture Iranian territory and trigger a revolt among non-Persian ethnic groups. (Iran is part of what was once the Persian Empire. Persians are not Arabs.) He thought that this revolt might lead to the collapse of the Iranian leadership.

In March 1980, Iraq ended diplomatic relations with Iran. The following month, Iraqi security forces expelled Shiite individuals suspected of collaborating with Iranian authorities. Thousands of people (some estimates say one hundred thousand) were expelled from Iraq, many for simply having a name of Persian origin. The government also provided financial incentives for Iraqi men to divorce their Iranian wives. Saddam justified this mass expulsion by saying, "Those who do not love Iraq and are not ready to shed blood in the defense of Iraqi territory and dignity, must leave Iraq." On September 17, 1980, Saddam renounced an earlier agreement with

SADDAM VISITS IRAQI TROOPS WHO ARE PREPARING TO INVADE IRAN
in September 1980.

Iran. By the terms of this agreement, Iraq and Iran shared the Shatt al-Arab waterway. On September 22, 1980, full-scale war began when the Iraqi air force attacked ten Iranian air bases.

To help raise Iraqi morale, Saddam compared the war with another conflict that had taken place around A.D. 636. At that time, the newly created Islamic empire was expanding. An Arab-Muslim army decisively defeated a Persian army at the Battle of Qadisiyah in southern Iraq. The Arab-Muslim victory led to the Islamic conquest of Persia. The Baath Party officially called the September 1980 battle against Iran Qadisiyyat Saddam (Saddam's Qadisiyah). During the war against Iran, Iraqi propaganda evoked images of the ancient battle to encourage citizens and soldiers. The message was that the Arab-Muslim victory against the Persians in the past could be achieved again in modern times.

Iraqi military leaders expected a short war ending in easy victory. By the end of the war's first week, it was clear that they had miscalculated. Instead of rapid progress onto Iranian territory, Iraqi forces had to fight very hard to make small gains. Iraqi casualties were much higher than expected. With a population one-third the size of Iran's, Iraq was less able to endure heavy losses. Still, at considerable cost, the Iraqis managed to capture the important Iranian oil-refining center of Khorramshahr on October 24, 1980. The fighting was so costly that both Iraqis and Iranians referred to Khorramshahr as the city of blood. This proved the high-water mark for the Iraqi offensive.

IRAQI TROOPS ADVANCE ON KHORRAMSHAHR IN OCTOBER 1980. THE smoke on the horizon is from burning oil along the Iranian pipelines.

Poor leadership hampered the Iraqi army. Saddam worried that successful military officers might plot to overthrow him. So he placed Baathist political commissars (political party officials whose job it is to ensure loyalty and obedience to party rules) in all military units. The commissars lacked military skills. Their only qualification was loyalty to Saddam. They gave political lectures, watched for signs of disloyalty, and interfered with military operations. Saddam also frequently rotated officers among different units so that the officers would not form bonds with their soldiers. Such rotations went against accepted worldwide military practice. In addition, Saddam entrusted almost all key command positions to loyal kinsmen. Consequently, the army did not perform well and the war's second phase featured a stalemate, with neither side able to make significant progress. The stalemate lasted until the spring of 1981, when Iran launched a series of attacks. During 1982 Iranian forces recaptured all Iranian territory taken by the Iraqis.

Saddam had staked his personal prestige on the outcome of the war with Iran. He was deeply troubled by the failure of his military to defeat Iran. Khomeini had convinced Iranians that the war against Saddam was a national crusade. The willingness of young Iranians to die for their cause alarmed Saddam. He looked for a way to pull out of the war. He hit upon the idea of stirring up trouble between Israel and the anti-Israeli Palestine Liberation Organization (PLO). He thought that he could provoke Israel into attacking the PLO in neighboring Lebanon. Then he could make peace with Iran and rally all Muslims against Israel. He used assassination as the tool to provoke Israel.

On the evening of June 3, 1982, three gunmen shot and seriously wounded the Israeli ambassador in London. The British captured the gunmen. Investigation later revealed that the assassins were members of a terrorist organization based in Baghdad. The weapons used by the assassins came from the Iraqi Embassy in London.

On June 6, 1982, the Israeli army invaded Lebanon just as Saddam had expected. Four days later, Saddam declared a ceasefire with Iran. He proposed to the Iranians that Iraq and Iran redirect their military resources against Israel. Iranian leader Ayatollah Khomeini rejected Saddam's proposal and ordered a new Iranian attack against Iraqi forces. Saddam's plan had failed.

AN ASSASSINATION ATTEMPT

By the end of the second year of the Iran–Iraq War, an estimated one hundred thousand Iraqis had died and uncounted thousands were injured. Inside Iraq, a militant Shiite group called the al-Dawa al-Islamiyah Party (the Call of Islam Party) chose this time to strike. Dawa is an underground organization that promotes a return to Islamic principles in the government and social justice for the people. The highly respected Shiite cleric Ayatollah Muhammad Bakr al-Sadr was the party's leader.

On April 1, 1980, Dawa tried to assassinate Saddam's information minister, Latif Jasim, and Deputy Prime Minister Tariq Aziz. The attempt failed. When Dawa struck again five days later, Saddam responded by making Dawa Party membership a crime punishable by death. He ordered the arrest and execution of Sadr and Sadr's sister, Amina Sadr (known to Shiites as Bint al-Huda). Then Saddam turned his wrath against the Shiites by ordering mass arrests. Many disappeared into the state prison never to be seen again.

WEAPONS OF
MASS DESTRUCTION

Saddam cast around for some other way to defeat Iran. He focused on unconventional weapons, such as poison gas, and increased efforts to obtain nuclear weapons. Iraqi scientists had promised Saddam that an Iraqi nuclear reactor used to produce electrical power would be ready to produce weapons-grade nuclear material

Dawa sought revenge by trying to kill Saddam. The attempt began on July 8, 1982, when Saddam was visiting the Shiite village of al-Dujail, about 40 miles (64 km) northeast of Baghdad. Saddam wanted to praise its people for contributing soldiers for the war against Iran. The assassins ambushed him and a two- to three-hour firefight ensued. The assassins failed to kill Saddam.

Saddam responded brutally. He sent his special security and military forces to carry out a reprisal attack against al-Dujail. Between 120 and 200 of the village's men were either killed in the massacre or executed later. About 1,500 more people were arrested and tortured. Other residents, including women and children, were sent to desert prison camps. Then the army destroyed the village.

The failed assassination attempt changed Saddam. Prior to it, his effort to portray himself as a man of the people led him to make many appearances around the country. Now those trips ended. Saddam was too worried about his personal safety.

by the summer of 1981. However, international pressure and the activities of Israeli secret agents had interfered with this schedule. Then, on June 7, 1981, Israeli aircraft destroyed the Iraqi nuclear reactor at al-Tuwaitha. However, most of the enriched uranium, the nuclear fuel used to power a nuclear bomb, had been stored safely underground. This allowed Saddam to restart the development of nuclear weapons.

Meanwhile, Iraqi scientists, with considerable assistance from East German scientists, worked hard at developing chemical and biological weapons. They tried to conceal what they were doing by claiming that construction projects were for academic research or for agricultural purposes. The first chemical weapons plant was finished in 1983. A newly created organization, the State Establishment for Pesticides Production, managed the plant. In fact, it produced poison gas for military use. Two more chemical weapons plants were completed by the end of 1986. By that time, Iraq possessed one of the largest chemical weapons manufacturing complexes in the world.

While Iraq developed weapons of mass destruction (WMD), Iran relied on its manpower advantage to press the fighting. Poorly trained and equipped Iranian forces met formidable Iraqi fortifications and suffered enormous losses. An Iraqi officer related how hard it was to fight against young Iranian soldiers who had no military skills but were brave and formidable: "My men are eighteen, nineteen, just a few years older than these [Iranian] kids. I've seen [my men] crying, and at times the officers have had to kick them back to their guns. Once we had Iranian kids on bikes cycling toward us, and my men started laughing, and then these kids started lobbing their hand grenades and we stopped laughing and started shooting."

THE TANKER WAR

The period of 1981 to 1984 witnessed what is known as the tanker war. Beginning in 1981, Iraqi forces had tried to destroy Iran's ability to export oil. In 1984 they expanded their efforts by attacking increasing numbers of oil tankers operating in the Persian Gulf. Using modern fighters and missiles purchased from France, in 1984 alone the Iraqis attacked seventy-one merchant ships. Beginning in April 1984, the Iranians responded with their own attacks against Iraqi merchant (cargo) ships. In addition, Iran threatened to prevent all tanker traffic by closing the Persian Gulf at a point called the Strait of Hormuz.

The tanker war became a major international incident for two reasons. According to one report, "Some 70 percent of Japanese, 50 percent of West European, and 7 percent of American oil imports came from the Persian Gulf in the early 1980s. Second, the assault on tankers involved neutral shipping as well as ships of the belligerent [warring] states." By early 1988, at least ten Western navies (including that of the United States) and eight regional navies were patrolling the area, in an attempt to ensure safe passage of oil tankers through the area.

Finally, the Iranians advanced onto Iraqi territory. The Iranian objective was to capture Basra, Iraq's second-largest city and the capital of Iraq's Shiite community. Although Iraqi soldiers had not fought particularly well during their invasion of Iranian territory, they performed much better defending their own soil. They fought with skill and determination and resisted repeated Iranian attacks. Between February 29 and March 1, 1984, one of the largest battles of the war took place. The two armies inflicted more than twenty-five thousand fatalities on each other.

From an Iraqi standpoint, the situation appeared desperate. In March 1984, when the Iranians captured the strategic Majnun Islands north of Basra, Saddam responded by unleashing his chemical weapons. For years Iran had protested Iraqi use of these weapons, but Iraq denied the allegations and the international community, most of whom initially sided with Iraq, ignored their existence. This time was different. Iraqi helicopters dropped gas-filled canisters on the Iranians at the Majnun Islands. A small electric pump inside the canisters triggered on impact to spread the gas. Other helicopters sprayed a greasy yellow liquid. Exposed Iranian soldiers fell ill immediately. They began vomiting. For some, their skin turned red. Others experienced skin blistering, and their faces turned black. Then they died.

A United Nations (UN) investigating team concluded that the Iraqis had employed mustard gas and a chemical nerve gas called tabun. German companies had developed tabun during World War II. Adolf Hitler (the leader of Nazi Germany) had refrained from using tabun on the battlefield. German scientists had taught Iraqi scientists how to manufacture tabun. But unlike Hitler, Saddam had used the deadly nerve gas.

After the chemical attack, the Iranians successfully employed protective gear and antidotes against Iraqi chemical weapons. The Iraqis, in turn, found the weapons difficult to use. Often the gas blew back into their faces and caused serious harm. Worse, from an Iraqi standpoint, the use of poison gas turned the once supportive international community against Iraq.

Undaunted, Saddam again expanded the war effort in the spring of 1985 by ordering his air forces to bomb civilian targets in Iran. Iran responded by bombarding Baghdad with missiles. For the next three years, fighting raged, but neither side saw decisive success in the war effort.

GASSING THE KURDS

Iraqi Kurds had hoped to take advantage of the war with Iran to achieve their dream of independence and a Kurdish nation. The Iranians supported this effort. In late May 1987, the war seemed to have reached a stalemate on the southern front. So Iranian forces, supported by Iraqi Kurdish rebels, attacked in the north. In a series of actions in Kurdistan (a region dominated by the Kurds, centered in the northern part of Iraq and including adjacent regions in Turkey and Iran), the Iranians and Kurdish rebels threatened Iraq's oil fields near Kirkuk and the vital northern oil pipeline to Turkey.

Saddam responded savagely. He ordered the execution of about eight thousand Kurdish prisoners. Then he sent his cousin, General Ali Hassan al-Majid to deal with the Kurds. General Ali moved the Kurds into new settlements in the southwestern Iraqi desert where they could not threaten Saddam's government. Ali's forces then destroyed the abandoned towns and villages. Estimates suggest that by 1988 half of all the villages in the Kurdish region of Iraq had been destroyed.

When the Kurds tried to resist this forced removal, Ali (who became known in the West as Chemical Ali) responded with chemical weapons. The first reported attacks had occurred in May 1987, when Iraqi forces used poison gas against Kurdish villages on the Iranian border. The most infamous incident occurred on March 16, 1988. Iraqi planes delivered a thick cloud of poison gas over the Kurdish village of Halabjah. About five thousand men, women, and children were killed. Another ten thousand suffered injuries including blindness. According to the U.S. State Department, "Iraqi soldiers in protective gear returned to Halabjah to study the effectiveness of their weapons and attacks. They divided the city into

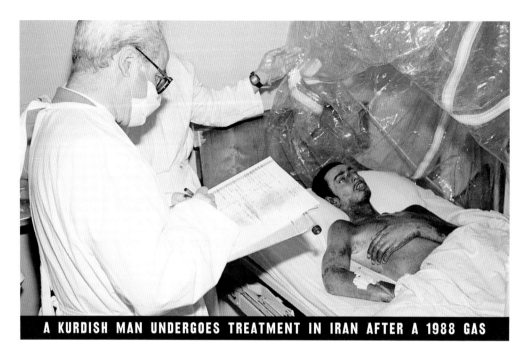

A KURDISH MAN UNDERGOES TREATMENT IN IRAN AFTER A 1988 GAS
attack by Iraqi forces in Halabjah, Iraq.

grids, determining the number and location of the dead and extent of injury. Halabjah helped Saddam Hussein gauge the ability of his chemical agents to kill, maim, and terrorize."

Saddam had authorized the first use of nerve gas on the battle-field when Iraqi helicopters gassed the Iranians at the Majnun Islands. He added to this dubious record by being the first ruler in history to use nerve gas against his own people.

THE IRAN–IRAQ WAR ENDS

By 1988 the Iraqi military had changed. In order to survive the Iranian onslaught, Saddam allowed professional military men to direct military actions. Baath Party commissars still kept close watch, but they did not interfere with strictly military operations. This was far different from the early war years when an atmosphere of distrust between the army and the party pervaded. In addition, instead of incompetent political appointees, professional military men were now in important command positions. The military was also better equipped. Several Persian Gulf countries, notably Kuwait and Saudi Arabia, had loaned Iraq huge sums of money for its war effort. Saddam used the money to purchase vast quantities of the most modern military equipment.

The improvement of the military was obvious during four major battles fought from April to August 1988. In the first battle, the Iraqi Republican Guard (an elite military unit) and regular army units recaptured Iraqi territory on the al-Faw Peninsula. The Iraqis effectively used chemical weapons against Iranian command and control facilities, artillery positions, and logistics points. In the subsequent three battles, the Iraqis routed or defeated the Iranians. On July 18, 1988, the UN Security Council passed a resolution calling for a cease-fire in the Iran–Iraq War. Fighting formally ended on August 20, 1988.

The precise human cost of the Iraq–Iran War is unknown. Neither side kept nor reported reliable figures. The war took place in a hot, humid climate where wounds easily became infected. Medical care on both sides was poor, so many wounded eventually died. Estimates of the total number of dead range from 500,000 to 1 million. European and American sources estimate that more than 375,000 Iraqis died during the war.

Regardless of the cost in human lives, Saddam declared victory. Saddam ordered a colossal memorial built to celebrate the victory. It was modeled after the Arc de Triomphe in Paris, France. Two huge bronze fists modeled after Saddam's own hands were embedded in concrete. The fists held a pair of giant, steel swords that crossed overhead to create an arch. The arch soared 131 feet (40 m) into the air. The swords were cast from melted-down weapons captured from the Iranians. Beneath each arm hung nets filled with helmets taken from the bodies of dead Iranian soldiers. On August 8, 1989, the day the arches were commemorated, Saddam made an appearance. He rode on a white stallion to evoke memories of the horse ridden by the grandson of the prophet Muhammad during a famous battle in 680. Saddam wore a white jacket with gold trim and a white helmet festooned with a white ostrich feather. This was the same uniform worn by Iraq's kings during official visits. Saddam rode beneath the arch as a demonstration of Iraq's power and ambition.

SADDAM'S WOMEN

During the later years of the war with Iran, Saddam experienced family problems. He had become bored with his wife Sajida. He developed a wandering eye and seemed particularly attracted to younger, blond women, preferably those who were married. Rumors said that he enjoyed humiliating their husbands. Saddam's wife objected to his behavior. She tried to enlist family members, including their son Uday, to convince him to stop.

By this time, however, Uday had become much like his father. According to Iraqi army officers, "[Uday] is rude and shows no respect. He is a bully and a thug." After listening to his mother's complaints about Saddam's womanizing and her warning that, if Saddam remarried, Uday would lose his inheritance, Uday took action. He killed the man who procured mistresses for his father. This act enraged Saddam.

SADDAM'S VICTORY ARCH WAS THE FOCAL POINT OF A CELEBRATION OF his self-proclaimed victory in the Iran–Iraq War—a war that cost Iraq hundreds of thousands of dead and hundreds of billions of dollars.

He personally beat Uday and then ordered him jailed. Saddam ordered Uday's wife removed from public view. Saddam ordered the killing of Sajida's brother, who served as defense minister. Then Saddam arranged to marry his favorite mistress.

Iraqi society permits men to have more than one wife at the same time. However, this was an awkward situation for a head of state. Saddam solved this problem by officially separating from Sajida. Still, as the mother of Uday, his firstborn son, and four other children, she deserved respect. Accordingly, Saddam gave her the title Lady of the Ladies. He then married his former mistress, Samira Shahbandar, in 1986. She was given the title First Lady. For the remainder of his life, Saddam continued to enjoy mistresses. It was also rumored that he had a total of four wives.

CHAPTER 4

THE
COALITION

DURING THE EIGHT-YEAR WAR WITH IRAN, Saddam's inability to defeat Iran militarily weakened his self-confidence. He became increasingly paranoid. He ordered an extraordinary number of fortified palaces built throughout Iraq. At least fifteen palaces were built within a 31-mile (50 km) radius in northern Iraq. Each palace had its own garden and orchard to provide food. A thick wall surrounded each palace to protect against missile attack. Special security forces provided permanent garrisons (groups of soldiers). Saddam had grown so fearful of assassination attempts that he seldom spent more than a few days in any one palace before moving to another. As an experienced assassin himself, he knew how assassination teams operated. He judged that his enemies could not attack him if they did not know where he was. Nonetheless, the period 1988 to 1990 featured several attempted assassinations.

VERSUS SADDAM

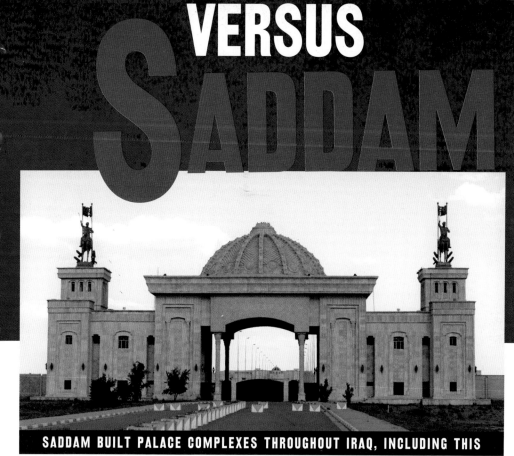

SADDAM BUILT PALACE COMPLEXES THROUGHOUT IRAQ, INCLUDING THIS
one in Tikrit. Each complex was gated *(above)* and had many buildings. Saddam
moved from palace to palace to avoid assassination.

The assassination attempts were a sign of the growing discontent with Saddam's rule. In 1988 Saddam Hussein had claimed victory in his war with Iran. However, the war had exhausted both the Iraqi people and the nation's economy. Iraq's infrastructure was in ruins. Roads, pipelines, irrigation systems, and power generating plants all needed repair. The nation was nearing bankruptcy. It depended on oil revenues to power the economy, yet half of those revenues had to be used to pay interest on war debt.

ECONOMIC FAILURE

Saddam tried to revive Iraq's economy. Price controls that had been installed during the war to prevent profiteering (making extravagant profits on the sale of essential goods) were removed. To allow more people to participate in the economy, the government sold about forty-seven state-run factories that produced foodstuffs, textiles, building materials, and aluminum to the private sector. It also enacted special policies to encourage small-business activity. The government disbanded peasants' cooperatives and sold state farms to private businessmen. It allowed farms to sell crops directly to wholesalers. It loosened import-export regulations and foreign exchange restrictions. Iraqi officials worked to attract foreign investment, particularly from nearby Gulf states.

These efforts at economic revival did not work. Saddam had never formally studied economics. He seldom listened to expert advice. Instead, he operated on instinct and impulse. The consequences were unsurprising. The removal of price controls led to inflation (rising prices). As a result, people living on fixed incomes, particularly government workers, saw the buying power of their salaries shrink month after month. Overall, only a small group of privileged businessmen grew richer. The rest of the country grew steadily poorer.

SADDAM-STYLE DIPLOMACY

At the same time, Saddam tried to mend his diplomatic fences. He persuaded many in the international community that a secular (nonreligious) and progressive Iraq under his leadership was better than having the region dominated by Iran and its fanatical religious zealots. Because some foreign powers feared what would happen if Iran defeated Iraq, they had supported Iraq during the war. The oil-producing Gulf states, most notably Saudi Arabia, Kuwait, and the United Arab Emirates, contributed an estimated $40 billion in covert (behind-the-scenes) support to Iraq. The United States also provided covert support. However, word of Saddam's dismal human rights record spread. In particular, Saddam's campaign against the Kurds angered many European powers, as well as the United States. Furthermore, Western intelligence agencies strongly suspected that Saddam was pressing ahead in his effort to acquire weapons of mass destruction, including nuclear weapons. Then an incident brought both the issues of human rights and WMD into sharper focus.

Farzad Bazoft was an Iranian-born journalist working in Iraq for the British newspaper The *Observer*. On September 19, 1989, citizens in Baghdad heard a powerful explosion from outside the city. Bazoft and other journalists working for the Western media tried to investigate. Although Saddam personally ordered the incident kept secret, information leaked out about what had happened.

The explosion came from a secret rocket assembly plant 30 miles (48 km) from Baghdad. Dozens of Egyptian technicians involved in developing a medium-range missile were killed. Bazoft apparently disguised himself and investigated. Iraqi security officers arrested him as he was trying to leave the country. They found he had taken photos of the secret site and was carrying soil samples. The Iraqis arrested Bazoft and held him in Abu Ghraib prison near Baghdad for six weeks, claiming that he was an Israeli spy.

The international community protested his arrest and detention. Saddam wrote a personal letter to British prime minister

Margaret Thatcher, assuring her that Bazoft would receive a fair trial. On November 1, 1989, Bazoft appeared on Iraqi television and confessed that he was an Israeli spy. He had undoubtedly been forced to make this confession. The court ordered him executed. In spite of international pleas for clemency (a milder sentence), Bazoft was executed by hanging on March 15, 1990.

Iraq's information minister, Latif Jasim, proudly noted that Prime Minister Thatcher "wanted him alive. We gave her the body." Immediately after Bazoft's execution, Iraq ordered Britain's ambassador to Iraq to leave the country and canceled high-level, official diplomatic contact with Great Britain.

Bazoft's execution was the last straw for some members of the international community. Particularly in the West, dismay over Iraq's lack of human rights and worry about Saddam's development of WMD combined to prevent Western powers from establishing normal relations with Iraq.

Scud was the name given to a series of missiles developed by the Soviet Union in the decades following World War II. The Soviets sold these missiles to many other countries, including Iraq. Scuds are small enough to be transported overland on specially equipped vehicles that also serve as launchers.

THE INVASION OF KUWAIT

Iraq emerged from the war against Iran with a military numbering more than one million men, an extensive arsenal of chemical weapons, extended-range Scud missiles, and a large air force. Its army was the fourth largest in the world. Its military was the premier armed force in the Persian Gulf region.

Saddam concluded that his growing unpopularity within and outside Iraq and the deteriorating Iraqi economy required drastic action. Efforts to reform the economy had caused steep price increases and an inflation rate estimated at 45 percent. Yet Saddam continued to authorize the spending of vast sums for prestige projects such as victory monuments and new presidential palaces. The military rearmament budget soared. Saddam even ordered the purchase of a small fleet of warships, although Iraq had neither a naval tradition nor a base to support a fleet.

Around the end of 1989, Saddam began planning to invade Kuwait. He thought that the invasion would distract the Iraqi people from their problems. He also judged that Kuwait would provide him a vast amount of money, which in turn would help rebuild the Iraqi economy.

Like Iraq, Kuwait was an artificial creation. In 1922 a British diplomat, Sir Percy Cox, had set the borders among Iraq, Kuwait, and Saudi Arabia. Cox had drawn a boundary that arbitrarily separated Iraq from Kuwait. From that time on, the boundary had been a source of Iraqi complaint. Furthermore, Kuwait had two things that Saddam coveted: a well-developed coastline providing better access to the Persian Gulf and a tremendous oil reserve. In addition, there were some particular border disputes. Iraqi oilmen believed that Kuwait was illegally tapping the large and valuable Rumaila oil field that lay beneath the Iraq–Kuwait border. Also, both Iraq and Kuwait wanted control of two islands just off the coast of southern Iraq.

Saddam had probably already decided to attack Kuwait, but on July 18, 1990, he demanded that Kuwait repay Iraq for oil it had allegedly stolen. He also demanded that Kuwait forgive Iraq's huge debt from the war with Iran. When Kuwait failed to oblige Saddam, the Iraqi military made final preparations for war. Kuwait had a small, sixteen-thousand-man army. On August 2, 1990, Saddam sent about one hundred thousand men and three hundred tanks against the Kuwaitis. The undermanned, underequipped Kuwaiti military hardly resisted. Within seven hours, the Iraqi military occupied the entire country and overthrew its government.

The international reaction to the Iraqi invasion surprised Saddam. Within hours U.S. president George H. W. Bush imposed economic sanctions (punishments). British prime minister Margaret Thatcher denounced Saddam's occupation of Kuwait, declaring, "Aggressors must never be appeased [pacified]." The UN Security Council imposed a total economic and trade embargo (prohibition) on Iraq. Even the Soviet Union, a longtime Saddam ally, and numerous Arab nations condemned the invasion. Most important, Saudi Arabia asked for U.S. military help in case Saddam sent his tanks in their direction. This request effectively invited the United States to establish military bases on Iraq's border.

On August 7, 1990, five days after the invasion, President Bush announced two demands that Iraq had to meet: immediate and unconditional withdrawal from Kuwait and the restoration of the legitimate Kuwaiti government.

Saddam responded to Bush the next day. Saddam said Iraq had annexed (permanently taken over) Kuwait. The Revolutionary Command Council, of course, endorsed Saddam. It announced on

August 29, 1990, that "what time had wronged" had been fixed by the invasion. The "injustice and unfairness that had hit Iraq" was resolved with the return of the "branch, Kuwait, to the whole and root, Iraq." The two were now one "in a comprehensive, eternal and inseparable merger." The RCC statement announced to the world that Kuwait had officially become Iraq's nineteenth province.

The United States assembled a coalition of forces that grew from twenty-eight members to thirty-seven members. Included were not only traditional U.S. allies such as Great Britain and Australia but also Egypt and Syria. On the eve of war with Iraq, more than seven hundred thousand soldiers, sailors, airmen, and marines were ready to liberate Kuwait. The U.S. contingent was by far the largest, with about five hundred thousand troops.

The Iraqi army had trained after the model of the Soviet Union. As a result of the Cold War (1945–1991)—during which the United States and the Soviet Union competed for influence over the rest of the world—the U.S. military had been preparing to fight Soviet ground forces. U.S. forces were therefore perfectly trained to fight the Iraqis. By any realistic measure, the Iraqi forces stood little chance of defeating the coalition. Professional Iraqi military men

COALITION TROOPS FROM THE United States cross the Saudi desert in 1990 in preparation for entering Kuwait.

understood this. Saddam did not. The professionals were too afraid to tell Saddam the truth.

Saddam, still surprised by the international response to his invasion of Kuwait, began to realize the likelihood of war with the coalition. So he invested his hopes for Iraqi success in some bizarre strategies. One was the use of human shields. Small numbers of antiwar activists from all over the world had gone to Iraq. Saddam's propaganda (ideas, facts, or allegations spread deliberately to further one's cause) machine used them as props during antiwar broadcasts. They were shown, side by side with Saddam, holding antiwar signs and shouting antiwar sentiments. Saddam hoped that these foreign peace activists would influence their home nations. He judged that if antiwar sentiment spread, foreign political leaders would be unwilling to wage war. When it became apparent that the coalition meant to end the Iraqi occupation of Kuwait, Saddam had the foreigners sent to strategic sites in Iraq and Kuwait. He thought that their presence would prevent the coalition from attacking these sites with bombs and missiles.

Saddam had always been able to terrify his citizens with boasts and threats. He tried the same tactic against the coalition. He proclaimed that if the coalition attacked Iraq, it would trigger "the mother of all battles." Meanwhile, the Iraqi military systematically looted Kuwait and brutalized the Kuwaiti people.

OPERATION DESERT STORM

Operation Desert Storm began on January 16, 1991. For more than five weeks, coalition forces blasted Iraqi positions from the air.

Saddam responded the way he had when the war with Iran went poorly: by trying to draw Israel into the war. During the Iran–Iraq War, his tactic was to attempt to assassinate the Israeli ambassador in London. This time, he ordered missiles fired at Israel. Once again, Israeli leaders refused to take Saddam's bait and responded with restraint. And again, Saddam's strategy failed.

In late January, Saddam ordered Kuwaiti oil installations set on fire. On January 25, he had crude oil pumped into the northern Persian Gulf in an attempt to deter the coalition's attack. His efforts created the largest oil slick in history, but it did nothing to deter the coalition. All Saddam could do was make preparations to ensure that he and his key lieutenants survived the war and hope that his ground forces could defeat the coalition. On February 23, 1991, coalition ground forces began their assault.

Under the leadership of U.S. general Norman Schwarzkopf, the coalition forces swept through the Iraqi defenses. Saddam had invested his hopes for victory in a line of fortifications across Kuwait. Called the Saddam Line, Saddam reasoned that such fortifications had stopped the Iranians during the previous war. This time, his enemies skillfully breached the Saddam Line in a matter of hours.

The battle turned into a rout as Iraqi forces fled Kuwait. In the war's waning hours, U.S. forces were herding Republican Guard units into a pocket against the Euphrates River near Basra. At the same time, the coalition air forces were attacking Iraqi convoys (groups of military vehicles) fleeing from the Kuwaiti capital of Kuwait City. They fled along the road that would soon be called the Highway of Death because of the number of Iraqi troops killed there. Television pictures showed images of destruction and carnage. In Washington, D.C., the Bush administration worried that these images gave the impression that U.S. forces were merely brutal killers.

The Bush administration decided that it had accomplished enough by liberating Kuwait from Iraqi occupation. The coalition would not go further and attempt to topple Saddam. So on February 28, 1991, exactly one hundred hours after the ground campaign began, President Bush announced the suspension of coalition attacks. It was just in time for the Republican Guard, who had not yet been completely surrounded and destroyed by the Americans. Bush's decision to halt the war allowed the survivors to escape.

By any measure, the Gulf War ended in catastrophe for Iraq. Coalition forces destroyed half the Iraqi army divisions they faced,

STRIPPING KUWAIT

Iraqi troops removed from Kuwait everything of value they could find: not just cars, computers, and jewels but even streetlights and school blackboards. Iraqi troops loaded medical equipment from hospitals and furniture and appliances from people's homes into military vehicles bound for Iraq. Soldiers also broke into stores, including Toys "R" Us, and helped themselves to the merchandise.

At the time of the invasion, Kuwait was a nation of two million people. Three hundred thousand of them fled the country during the Iraqi occupation. Those who remained lived in fear as the occupying army swept through Kuwait and randomly arrested thousands of people. Some were tortured and imprisoned. Some were executed and their bodies dumped near their homes. Hundreds of others were never seen again. Families of the executed were forced to pay for the bullets used to kill their loved ones.

killing an estimated one hundred thousand Iraqis and capturing another sixty thousand. A U.S. general famously boasted, "Iraq went from the fourth-largest army in the world to the second-largest army in Iraq in 100 hours."

As had been the case after the war with Iran, Saddam held a different opinion. From his perspective, he had survived attack by the world's combined military might. Moreover, enough Republican Guard units remained to keep him in power.

REBELLION

The greatest threat to Saddam came after the end of Operation Desert Storm. For the first time since he had begun his reign, his own people rose in rebellion. The rebellion started in the Shiite south, around the city of Basra. It quickly spread to al-Najaf and Karbala. A female rebel described the scene in Karbala: "With makeshift weapons and our own bodies, we began to confront the Iraqi soldiers who had entered the town in recent days yet who were already weakened by weeks of allied bombing, desertions, and the army's withdrawal from Kuwait. The soldiers started firing on the crowd—the first time I had ever seen live shooting. Caught up in the frenzy of noise and excitement, I didn't run for cover. Instead, I kept shouting along with the others, 'Down with Saddam!' Years of anger within me came pouring out." Encouraged by the Shiite success, the Kurds in the north also rebelled. Soon the Kurdish rebels controlled almost all of Kurdistan.

Delegates from twenty-three exiled Iraqi opposition groups met in Beirut, Lebanon, on March 10, 1991, to plan a coordinated strategy against Saddam. However, none of the major powers strongly backed the overthrow of Saddam. The leaders of the oil-rich Gulf states, all of whom were Sunni, feared what would happen if Saddam were removed. They worried that Iran would enter southern Iraq to take over that region's oil resources. This would create a powerful Shiite community that the Sunni leaders did not welcome. In the north, Turkey opposed the creation of an independent Kurdish state, which would take some of its territory. In turn, the United States did not want to upset its ally, Turkey, or its allies among the Persian Gulf monarchies, particularly Saudi Arabia—a major supplier of oil to the United States. Consequently, the rebels inside Iraq had to fight against Saddam without support from foreign powers. This lack of foreign support provided Saddam with the chance to crush them.

Saddam cunningly made sure that he gave the coalition powers no reason to intervene in Iraq's internal affairs. His foreign minister, Tariq Aziz, negotiated with the UN to settle the terms of the Gulf War cease-fire. Saddam authorized Aziz to yield to enough UN demands to satisfy the international community. Among the demands, Iraq was to allow UN inspections that were intended to monitor Iraqi compliance with restrictions on weapons development. (However, Iraq allowed only a few of the inspections.) Then Saddam consolidated his hold inside the government by promoting key deputies whom he completely trusted. Consequently, his favorite son-in-law, Hussein Kamel al-Majid, became minister of defense; his longtime friend Taha Ramadan became deputy president; and Ali Hassan al-Majid, the officer who had supervised the chemical attacks against the Kurds, became minister of the interior. Having surrounded himself with dependable deputies, Saddam sent his forces against the rebels.

Saddam's best and most loyal soldiers, the Republican Guard, attacked Shiite strongholds in al-Najaf and Karbala. They arrested Shiite clerics and summarily executed hundreds of them. The Republican

Guard tied civilians to tanks, using them as human shields, so the rebels would not fight back. Leaders called in helicopters to attack civilians. After Saddam's forces were done, they allowed Western journalists to survey their handiwork. A British journalist reported that "Karbala looked as if it had been hit by an earthquake."

THE MARSH ARABS

Southern Iraq historically featured great stretches of marsh and shallow water. Tall reed fields grew up from the water and provided a unique environment. The marshes supported a rich diversity of waterfowl and other aquatic life. It was the ancestral home for the Ma'dan, also called the Marsh Arabs. The Marsh Arabs had inhabited this region for more than five thousand years. They lived on small islands and moved about by pushing their sharp-prowed boats along paths through the reeds. Their livelihood relied on fishing, water buffalo, and small livestock herds.

In 1991 an estimated 250,000 Marsh Arabs lived in Iraq. They were mostly Shiite and consequently had been oppressed by the Sunni-dominated Baath Party. In addition, since the Marsh Arabs lived in a remote place, the marshes became a sanctuary for Saddam's opponents. This made the region a special target for Saddam's security forces.

According to Human Rights Watch—an international human rights organization—"Marsh Arabs have been singled out for even more direct assault: mass arrests, enforced 'disappearances,' torture, and execution of political opponents have been accompanied by ecologically catastrophic drainage of the marshlands and the large-scale and systematic forcible transfer of part of the local population."

The campaign against the Marsh Arabs featured a massive effort to eliminate the marshes themselves. Government water control projects drained most of the inhabited marsh areas by drying up or diverting the feeder streams and rivers. The consequences were disastrous for the region's people and the environment. Marshes dried up, salination (the build up of salt) and sedimentation (the build up of sand and dirt) increased, and neither the Marsh Arabs nor wildlife could continue to live as they always had. Worse followed.

Saddam ordered the construction of a 300-mile-long (483 km) channel, called Saddam's River, to divert water from the marsh. Middle East Watch—a branch of Human Rights Watch—reported, "At times whole families were deported, including children, aged parents and other relatives." An estimated two hundred thousand Shiites were expelled. Tariq Aziz candidly explained the efforts against the Marsh Arabs to a Western journalist, "We had a fifth column [an antigovernment force]. They [the Marsh Arabs] were of Persian origin. We said to them, 'You love Khomeini. Go back to his paradise.' We put them on trucks and sent them to the border."

The Marsh Arabs realized that Saddam's River threatened their entire way of life. In the summer of 1991, they revolted against the government. The governments of the United States, Great Britain, and France imposed a no-fly zone at the 33rd Parallel over southern Iraq to protect the Marsh Arabs. Any Iraqi airplane that entered the zone would be shot down by the allies' warplanes.

The no-fly zone did not deter Saddam. He understood that helicopter flights and ground operations could still take place in the zone. He sent soldiers backed by helicopters against the Marsh Arabs with orders to crush the rebellion. His military used conventional and chemical weapons to kill the Marsh Arabs and destroy their homes. According to Human Rights Watch, "In their attempt to retake cities, and after consolidating control, loyalist forces killed thousands of unarmed

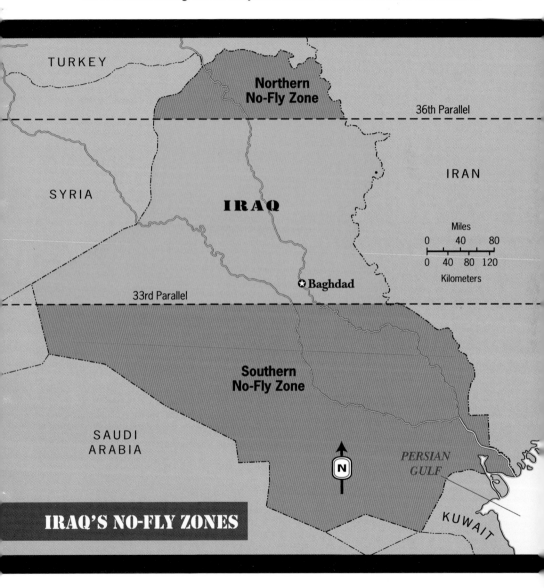

TURKEY

Northern
No-Fly Zone

36th Parallel

IRAN

SYRIA

IRAQ

Miles
0   40   80

0   40   80   120
Kilometers

33rd Parallel

☆ Baghdad

Southern
No-Fly Zone

SAUDI
ARABIA

PERSIAN
GULF

KUWAIT

IRAQ'S NO-FLY ZONES

civilians by firing indiscriminately into residential areas; executing young people on the streets, in homes and in hospitals; rounding up suspects, especially young men, during house-to-house searches, and arresting them without charge or shooting them *en masse*; and using helicopters to attack unarmed civilians as they fled."

By the time Iraqi forces completed their operations, the Marsh Arab population had been reduced from an estimated 250,000 to 40,000. A satellite image taken by the National Aeronautics and Space Administration (NASA) revealed that the marshes shrank by 90 percent. It was a human and an environmental catastrophe.

THE KURDS

Saddam's forces also attacked the rebellious Kurds. Here, too, the forces employed their usual tactics of terror and brutality. By the end of April 1991, an estimated two million Kurds had fled from the Iraqi troops. The refugees took shelter in the mountains between Kurdistan and Iran. They suffered terribly, with an estimated one thousand people starving to death each day.

The United States and Great Britain intervened to

A KURDISH MAN CARRIES HIS daughter over the Iraq–Turkey border as he flees Saddam's regime in 1991.

A UNIQUE PEOPLE

The Kurds are an ethnic minority distinct from the Arabs. They are an ancient Indo-European people. Historically, they have lived in the area where modern Turkey, Syria, Iraq, and Iran converge. Russia also has a Kurdish population. The Kurds speak their own language and observe different customs from the Arabs. In Iraq they live in the north around the urban centers of Mosul and Kirkuk. Almost all Kurds are Sunni Muslims. The Kurds have periodically revolted in an effort to achieve an autonomous (independent) state. Since the imposition of the no-fly zone in northern Iraq after the Gulf War, the Kurds have come close to achieving independence. More than any other group in Iraq, they have enjoyed relative peace and prosperity since 1991.

establish safe havens for the Kurds. Iraqi aircraft were forbidden from flying north of the no-fly zone set at the 36th Parallel. The United States and Great Britain then launched Operation Provide Comfort on April 6, 2001. This relief operation delivered tons of food, clothes, and tents for the desperate refugees.

By spring 1991, Saddam Hussein's regime had lasted longer than any other government since Iraq became an independent nation in 1932. Saddam could take satisfaction that he had weathered another crisis and emerged even stronger. He was particularly pleased the following year when President George H. W. Bush, the key leader of the international coalition that had fought Saddam, failed to win reelection. When Americans went to the polls in November 1992, the image of a swaggering, boastful Saddam still in power weighed heavily on voters' minds and contributed to Bush's defeat.

SADDAM VERSUS THE UN INSPECTORS

The next challenge Saddam confronted involved his unconventional weapons stockpile—the WMD. The UN Security Council had decided that Iraq should not have another opportunity to launch a war of aggression. It ordered Iraq to formally recognize Kuwait's independence, to repay Kuwait for all the damage the war had caused, and to allow UN inspectors free access in Iraq. These inspectors had the task of searching for evidence of Iraqi WMD programs. If the inspectors found such evidence, they were to make sure that the weapons were destroyed. The UN-imposed economic embargo against Iraq was to continue until the inspectors completed their work.

For seven years, the UN Special Commission on Iraq (UNSCOM) labored to unravel Iraq's WMD programs. Saddam's effort to hide these programs from the inspectors defeated UNSCOM. By the time UNSCOM departed, the inspectors had to admit that they did not know Iraq's capacity for manufacturing and delivering WMD.

Meanwhile, the Iraqi economy fell apart under the weight of UN-imposed sanctions. Iraq was particularly vulnerable to such sanctions because it relied heavily on imports. Two-thirds of the country's food, as well as a considerable proportion of technical and medical equipment, were imported. Saddam selectively allowed foreign reporters to witness people suffering from disease and malnutrition. He thought such publicity would force the UN to remove its sanctions. Indeed, the situation became so bad that in 1992 the UN offered the Iraqi government the opportunity to sell $1.6 billion worth of oil to purchase food and medicine. Saddam refused.

Instead, Saddam's security forces built an elaborate smuggling network to sell oil illegally on the black market (illegal trade in goods and commodities). Proceeds went to finance Saddam's regime. Finally, in May 1996, Saddam agreed to accept a new UN oil-for-food offer because it would bring more money into Iraq than the previous offer. By the terms of UN Security Resolution 986, Iraq was allowed to sell $2 billion worth of oil every six months and use the proceeds to buy food and medicine. The Oil for Food program failed miserably. Corruption at both ends undermined the program. UN officials made private deals to line their own pockets. Iraqi officials did the same.

Moreover, the program allowed Saddam to tighten his control over his people. Food from the Oil for Food program was distributed through about fifty-three thousand local grocery stores. People had to present a ration card to receive the food. Applicants for the ration cards had to provide detailed information to the government about their households. This information provided Saddam's security services with an updated database about the civilian population. Individuals were allowed to use their ration cards only within certain areas to cut down on local travel. In the minds of the Iraqi security service officials, travel restrictions reduced the likelihood that people would be able to plot and spread rebellion against Saddam.

Saddam also used the money from the oil sales to buy his subjects' loyalty. For example, loyal bureaucrats received new computers. Taxi drivers received new vehicles at greatly reduced prices. However, the government handouts to select people failed to match inflation or to significantly address the scarcity of food and other supplies caused by the international trade sanctions.

CHAPTER 5

TOOLS OF THE

WHEN SADDAM HUSSEIN BECAME PRESIDENT OF IRAQ in 1979, his goal was to create a totalitarian, one-party state based on his own cult of personality. From 1979 until his flight from Baghdad in 2003, every Iraqi institution worked to magnify his achievements. Iraqi television news broadcasts began each night with a scene of victorious soldiers and bursting fireworks accompanied by what Iraqis called the Saddam song:

> Oh Saddam, our victorious
> Oh Saddam, our beloved;
> You carry the nation's dawn
> Between your eyes.
> Oh Saddam, everything is good
> With you.

Allah! Allah! [*Allah* is Islam's word for "God."] We are happy;
Because Saddam lights our days.

PROPAGANDA

Television, radio, and newspapers produced countless stories
to glorify Saddam. Every day the newspapers featured a front-
page photo of Saddam, regardless of whether there was a story to
accompany it. Iraqi state and Baath Party propagandists used every
available modern information technique to burnish Saddam's cult
of personality. The poets, writers, and artists who worked to shape
Saddam's myth took ancient Iraqi symbols and recast them for a

THE IRAQI PRESS

The U.S. Constitution ensures freedom of the press. The press is viewed as a watchdog over the government's three branches (executive, legislative, and judicial). This was not so in Iraq once the Baath Party took over. Throughout the 1960s, the government heavily censored the press. It eventually banned almost all foreign publications. In 1969 it passed a law making the broadcast media the fourth branch of government so that the government could control the media. The government said that the media's most important goal was to convert the public to Baathism. Once Saddam became president, the media were to glorify him while mocking his enemies. No scientific or critical articles were written or broadcast on television or radio, and absolutely no humor making fun of the government was allowed. Instead, the media were full of poems praising Saddam or reports of military triumphs over Saddam's enemies.

modern mass media market. They took metaphors used in times past to describe Islamic rulers and applied them to Saddam. He was described as a lion or an eagle, as gold, or as a fortress. Other metaphors described him with images of light and rain or a flower or a tree in paradise.

They also relied on time-honored approaches with poets, writers, religious leaders, and professional propagandists glorifying Saddam while vilifying (making slanderous statements against) his enemies. This children's song, composed by an Iraqi poet, is a typical example:

We are Iraq and its name is Saddam;

We are love and its name is Saddam;

We are a people and its name is Saddam;

We are the Ba'ath and its name is Saddam.

Saddam directed his information ministry to create a new Iraqi history. Saddam did not care that the new history contradicted recorded historical facts. In the new, fabricated history, Iraq's ancient peoples were called Arabs. In fact, the Sumerians, Assyrians, and Babylonians lived in the land that became Iraq long before Arabs came to dominate the territory. Official propaganda compared Saddam to ancient leaders such as Nebuchadnezzar and Hammurabi. The propaganda altered the biographies of these historical figures in order to fit the new history. Saddam's vision was to create a myth that glorified Iraq's ancient past and then compare himself favorably to that past. Saddam's goal was to use himself as a symbol to unite his diverse country. In fact, at the 1988 Babylon International Festival, held at reconstructed ancient ruins outside of Baghdad, the festival emblem showed the profile of Saddam overlapping the profile of Nebuchadnezzar. The festival's slogan was "From Nebuchadnezzar to Saddam Hussein, Babylon arises anew." Teachers bombarded their students with stories designed to build the myth of the great Saddam.

A new genealogy was invented for Saddam. At one point, he was linked with the caliph al-Mansur, who ruled from A.D. 754 to 775. Al-Mansur had suppressed the Shiites while building Baghdad, so, in Saddam's mind, al-Mansur was a good role model. In 1985, during the height of the war against Iran, an article proclaimed, "Saddam [Hussein] al-Mansur will continue to be [our] moon and Iraq will be the flag of victory." The reference to al-Mansur had two meanings: literally it meant "victorious by the grace of Allah." It also elevated Saddam to the height of the great caliph.

Saddam's image and name were everywhere. A large part of Iraq's printing industry produced nothing but posters of Saddam. From the beginning to the end of his rule, posters provided images that connected Saddam with past Iraqi and Arab achievements. Giant paintings standing 20 feet (6 m) high supplemented the posters. They were part of the effort to reinforce the myth that Saddam was an all-seeing and all-knowing leader. They also portrayed him in different clothes. At Baghdad University, his portrait depicted him as a young graduate in cap and gown, even though he had never completed his university studies. In the Shiite city of Basra, he appeared as a peasant cutting wheat. At the racetrack in Baghdad, he was depicted as a desert horseman. In 1983 a German journalist reported, "It is scarcely possible to walk the streets here without encountering a photograph or larger than life poster of Saddam." The portraits aimed to build a myth that bonded the people strongly to Saddam.

When citizens met Saddam, he usually asked them how they were. The only proper

IRAQIS WAIT FOR A BUS BENEATH a mural of Saddam in Baghdad.

response was "as long as Saddam is well and strong, all Iraqis are well and prosperous." Numerous public places were named for him. A permanent exhibit dedicated to his life was built in Baghdad. Authorized biographers wrote about his life, fabricating details and glorifying his achievements. A special edition of the leading Baghdad newspaper featured a greatly revised version of his life story.

Saddam continually portrayed himself as a role model for Iraqis. Newspapers celebrated his devotion to his family. Iraqi children learned in school about Saddam's modest hobbies of fishing and gardening. Iraqi television showed Saddam making frequent surprise visits to factories, farms, and schools. He handed out patronage, or rewards, to "deserving" people.

JOB SECURITY

The Baath Party understood that its ability to provide jobs kept people loyal and satisfied. Between 1972 and 1978, the number of people employed by the state doubled. By 1978 the state directly employed an estimated 662,000 people. This figure did not include the military or security services. The Ministry of Interior alone employed more people than worked in large industrial enterprises. Most of its workers were charged with internal surveillance (keeping a close eye on Iraqis to guard against rebellion) and security (of Saddam and other top party officials).

After Saddam took control, this trend continued. Oil revenues that went straight to the Iraqi government allowed the state to play the determining role in the economy. This allowed "an unparalleled growth in the might of the state and of its apparatus of coercion and surveillance. Never before had the police and security forces in Iraq (or elsewhere in the Arab world) enjoyed such limitless powers." After the Gulf War, the state employed an estimated one in five members of the working class.

Saddam used Iraq's oil wealth to spread his patronage and purchase loyalty. Businessmen who were loyal to the Baath Party received government contracts. Iraq's private sector took advantage of the state's development projects, particularly in the areas of urban real estate, construction, transportation, and communications. However, projects that required high levels of technical ability that were lacking in Iraq, including major infrastructure and high-technology schemes, went to international companies. Nonetheless, Iraqi business owners found that even here they could earn fortunes by acting as go-betweens to link international firms with local subcontractors.

WELFARE STATE

Saddam also used Iraq's oil wealth to create a generous welfare state. By 1990 an estimated 40 percent of Iraqi households depended on government payments. Under his leadership, Iraq changed from a poor, agricultural nation into a bustling, developing country. The riches were spread unevenly, however. Baghdad featured all the trappings of a modern city: glass and steel hotels, newly constructed condominium towers, multilane highways, and fancy restaurants and casinos. In rural areas, particularly in the Shiite south, government projects were less common, so the inhabitants continued to live in hardship as they had in the past.

Because of the UN economic sanctions, the Iraqi government's education and welfare services eroded during the 1990s. The government lacked the money to fund these services. A shadow state replaced many government services. The shadow state was an unofficial network of patronage and violence run by Saddam's extended family. The network had little interest in providing goods and services to the people. Rather, it was much like a criminal network—its goal was to make money illegally for its members. This criminal-like shadow network came to dominate both official and unofficial Iraqi institutions.

REPRESSION

Saddam knew well Iraq's history of violent political change. Since he himself had served the Baath Party as an assassin, he understood that his own life was always in danger. Soon after becoming president in 1979, he told a guest, "I know that there are scores of people plotting to kill me, and this is not difficult to understand. . . . However, I am far cleverer than they are. I know they are conspiring to kill me long before they actually start planning to do so. This enables me to get them before they have the faintest chance of striking at me."

To avoid being assassinated and to maintain power, Saddam handed out generous rewards to loyalists and harsh punishments to anyone suspected of being an enemy. To preserve his rule, he exploited Iraq's ethnic, religious, and tribal divisions by systematically persecuting Shiites and Kurds. Saddam employed such tools as forced resettlement and unequal distribution of food and medicine to repress those he viewed as his enemies. His regime operated outside international principles regarding the rule of law and human rights. Instead, it employed secret arrests, detention without trial, torture, and executions of all opponents and any suspected opponents.

Most international law governs the relations of nations with one another. International human rights law regulates the relationship between a government and its citizens. In theory, human rights apply to everyone. They are universal. So nations have no excuse, in theory, for abusing human rights. Yet many do and organizations such as Human Rights Watch, Amnesty International, and others monitor abuses and report on them to put international pressure on nations to change their ways.

SECRET POLICE AND THE MILITARY

During Saddam's reign, he steadily expanded the secret police. Saddam always took care to choose close family members or trusted friends to head the security agencies. With so many agents, many had nothing better to do than spy on one another. Formally, the various secret police groups reported to the Revolutionary Command Council, which reported directly to Saddam. Saddam always took a keen interest in these reports.

The secret police had four main branches. The State Internal Security dealt with security matters inside Iraq, such as surveillance to identify political opposition. The Military Intelligence Agency directed operations outside Iraq. Its major target was Iraqi exiles living on foreign soil. To accomplish its work, the Military Intelligence Agency set up offices inside the military attaché's office of Iraqi embassies throughout the world. From this office, agents watched Iraqi exiles, citizens working abroad, and students. Sometimes exiles spoke against Saddam's government. From time to time, agents assassinated such exiles. The assassinations served

SADDAM *(CENTER)* MEETS WITH THE REVOLUTIONARY COMMAND COUNCIL and regional leadership of the Baath Party in Iraq. As head of these groups, Saddam had the mechanisms to stay in power.

as a warning to Iraqis living abroad that they were still within Saddam's reach.

A third branch of the secret police served as Saddam's personal security guards. It was called the Special Security. It operated in even greater secrecy than the other security organizations. It was headquartered in Saddam's presidential palace in Baghdad.

The fourth branch was the Intelligence Department, which acted as the security arm of the Baath Party. The Intelligence Department supervised all the other secret police organizations, as well as government ministries and selected popular institutions such as women's groups and youth groups. The Intelligence Department existed to ensure that no antigovernment speech or activity took place. It was the most powerful security organization in Iraq.

The Baath Party itself was a vital tool Saddam employed to stay in power. In the words of journalist Elaine Sciolino, "Over the years, Saddam had made the Party an instrument of his personal rule, transforming it into a mass organization to mobilize, indoctrinate, and control the people." The party grew from a small organization with only a few hundred full members in 1963 to an estimated 25,000 to 50,000 full members in 1990. In 1990 the party also had an estimated 1.5 million lower-level members.

The party maintained a strict hierarchy, meaning that only the most long-term, trusted members held leadership positions. It recruited among the nation's young people to form their ideas at an early age. Recruiters and teachers urged students to join Baath Party youth groups. They encouraged children to compete in displays of allegiance to Saddam. At the age of ten, candidates became members of the youth Vanguard and attended summer camps for military-style training. At the age of fifteen, they graduated to formal youth organizations. A recruit received special credit if he or she informed on a family

A YOUNG IRAQI GIRL SHOUTS PATRIOTIC SLOGANS AT A CELEBRATION FOR
Baath Party youth in 2002.

member who criticized Saddam. A party recruit could apply for party membership at the age of seventeen. That person then had to spend a minimum of seven and a half years working toward full membership. A recruit passed through stages known as sympathizer, supporter, candidate, and trainee before becoming a full working member.

Baath Party members thoroughly embedded themselves in Iraqi society. They were in schools, workplaces and, most importantly, in the military. Their presence created an atmosphere of constant surveillance and fear throughout Iraqi society.

The Iraqi military also served as an instrument to crush internal rebellions. Time and again, it proved itself better able and more willing to fight poorly armed or unarmed citizens than to fight foreign soldiers. Saddam was always deeply suspicious of his military,

Baathism is a strictly goal-oriented political ideology (system of thought; philosophy). It pays no attention to the human condition and does not recognize universal moral values. Only the party defines what is legitimate. Everything has a purpose, but that purpose is solely based on goals and objectives defined by the party. Saddam explained this to party militants: "Remember always the principles and experiences which are special to you are the only ones that represent final truth and which are able to respond to the task of building the new society for the Arab nation."

knowing that it had the potential to overthrow his government. So, like the Soviet dictator Joseph Stalin (1879–1953), he installed Baath Party commissars throughout the army. Their job was to spy on members of the military to detect plots and ensure loyalty.

To supplement the regular army, Saddam created a national militia (citizen army) in 1970 called the Popular Army. This army helped guard strategic sites and provided some border security. However, its only real purpose was to serve as another watchdog guarding against threats to Saddam's rule.

During the 1980s, Saddam formed the Republican Guard. At first this elite military corps served as a presidential bodyguard while also guarding Saddam's palaces and other strategic sites. After the 1991 Gulf War, the Special Republican Guard assumed these duties. Meanwhile, the Republican Guard expanded rapidly. By the early 2000s, it was the most powerful military force in Iraq, numbering between eighty thousand and one hundred thousand soldiers.

All soldiers in the Republican Guard were volunteers. Unlike the regular army with its Kurd and Shiite members, most Republican Guard were Sunnis and therefore more loyal to Saddam. The Republican Guard became Iraq's best-equipped and best-trained military force. Its officers and men received better pay and superior benefits compared to the regular army.

INFORMERS

According to a scholarly journal, Saddam "based his survival on the regime's ability to atomize [divide] Iraq's civil society, including the family unit, and in turning many Iraqis into accomplices and oppressors." A key part of this strategy was to encourage citizens to spy and inform on one another.

For example, the General Directorate of Security reviewed job applications, applications to acquire a sales license, and applications to practice a profession. Unless the applicant agreed to cooperate with the General Directorate of Security by informing on his or her fellow workers, the application was turned down. The General Directorate of Security made one more request before approving an application. It requested that the applicant write an initial report about any information he had on Baathist political opponents, sabo-teurs (those who engage in acts of destruction against a govern-ment), and deserters. If the directorate judged that the applicant had written a good report, it approved the application.

As a result, individual Iraqis lived in constant fear that someone would inform on them. Especially terrifying was the prospect that informants didn't need to provide proof of their claims. The conse-quences of being informed on included arrest, beatings, torture, and death. Everyone suspected that informers were everywhere. In a Baath Party document published in 1977, Saddam instructed the nation's teachers to teach children to be wary of all foreigners. The combination of years of such propaganda and fear of state author-ity all but eliminated traditional Arab hospitality. Foreign journalists assigned to Iraq observed that citizens were too fearful to speak with them. Elaine Sciolino wrote, "Hospitality was dangerous, and the foreigner, particularly the probing journalist, was regarded as an unwelcome intruder." Diplomats commented that they could spend three years in the country and never get to know a single Iraqi on a personal basis. A European diplomat observed, "There is a feeling that at least three million Iraqis are watching the eleven million others."

TORURE

After 1975 state authority expanded enormously. Russian and East German instructors visited Iraq to teach authorities torture tech-niques. The ultimate purpose of torture was not to obtain informa-tion. It was to create an atmosphere of fear. Iraqi citizens knew that authorities could seize and torture them at any time. In the words of Iraqi historian Kanan Makiya, "The range of cruel institutional practices in contemporary Iraq—confession rituals, public hangings, corpse displays, executions, and finally torture—are designed to breed and sustain widespread fear."

A 1978 report from Amnesty International, an international human rights organization, stated, "Almost all those who are arrested are reported to be tortured." The torture victim confronted a terrible choice: continue to endure pain, often to the brink of death, or confess. If the victim confessed, however, he or she would be executed. A female torture victim described her torturers: "They are experts at keeping the ones they are questioning one breath away from death. It is a game for them to see if they can push and pull a human back and forth, in and out of the grave."

A common practice of the Iraqi security forces was to force a male prisoner to watch his wife and children be raped. Then the prisoner was given a choice: either confess or witness even more family members receive the same treatment. Iraqi exiles also experienced this practice. If an exile began to talk openly about what was happening in Iraq, he would receive a package in the mail. The package would contain a film shot in Iraq of Iraqi security forces raping someone in the exile's family. The package also contained a warning: shut up or else.

A former prisoner submitted testimony to Amnesty International regarding his treatment at Abu Ghraib prison, where he was held from May 1982 to March 1984. He described what took place in the prison's torture chambers: "Torture takes the form of electric shocks; gas and cigarette burns; electric hot plates; hanging from the ceiling—handcuffed; being stretched on a special machine with hands and feet bound; beatings with a heavy cable or high pressure hose."

A TALE OF TORTURE

In December 1979, the Committee against Repression and for Democratic Rights in Iraq, a British-based organization, published the testimony of Barham Shawi, a twenty-two-year-old poet and essayist from the Iraqi town of Kut:

> I thought I would never be able to write again after they came close to cutting off my fingers by burning, stamping or thrashing them with sticks. . . . I was also caned and flayed until my feet were swollen. These rounds of hard group beating were interspersed by orders to leap and trot on the same spot I was in . . . they crucified me on the floor and nailed me there by stepping on my palms and arms. . . . My thighs were ripped apart violently and they began to rape me.

A female prisoner described torture at the notorious al-Baladiyat secret police headquarters in Baghdad: "The cell door was opened with great force. I cringed, believing that I was going to be taken away for further beatings. Instead, a woman who had been tortured almost to death was thrown to the floor. Her face was raw with deep cuts, and her skull had been cracked. Blood oozed from a hole in her head that appeared to have been made by an electric drill. Three of her lower fingernails had been ripped out, and so many cigarettes had been put out on her legs that the stench of burnt flesh soon filled the cell."

In the early 1980s, an Iraqi opposition group submitted a report to the UN that described what was taking place inside Iraq: "The dictatorship of Saddam Hussein is one of the harshest, most ruthless and most unscrupulous regimes in the world. It is a totalitarian, one-party system based on the personality cult of Saddam Hussein. This man and his family and relatives have control over the regular army, People's Army, police and security services. All news media are under the strict control of the regime and there is no opportunity for freedom of expression. Political organization is limited to the Baath Party and a number of insignificant . . . organizations. Trade unions do not exist. Membership in an opposition party is punishable by death. Any criticism of the President is also punishable by death. Torture is the norm. The security system is . . . omnipresent, and enjoys unlimited powers."

A decade later, little had changed. The UN issued a report dated April 5, 1991, condemning Saddam Hussein's use of the military and secret police to oppress the Iraqi civilian population: "Saddam Hussein has expanded his violence against women and children; continued his horrific torture and execution of innocent Iraqis; continued to violate the basic human rights of the Iraqi people and has continued to control all sources of information (including killing more than 500 journalists and other opinion leaders in the past decade). Saddam Hussein has also harassed humanitarian aid workers; expanded his crimes against Muslims; he has withheld food from families."

THE U.S. GOVERNMENT ESTIMATES IRAQ'S POPULATION in the early 2000s to be about 26.7 million people. About 75 to 80 percent of the population are Arab Muslims. The second-largest ethnic group is the Kurds, who comprise about 15 to 20 percent of the population. The balance of the population consists mainly of descendants from ancient invasions and long-past civilizations. They include the Turkomans, Persians, Christian Armenians, and Chaldean and Assyrian Christians. Traditionally Iraq had been home to a sizable Jewish population of about 150,000. Persecution against the Jews began in 1951, and almost all Jews fled the country.

Ninety-seven percent of Iraq's population are Muslims. This figure includes the Kurds. The overwhelming majority of Kurds are Sunni Muslims. Among the rest of the Muslim population, about 60 to 65 percent are Shiite and 32 to 37 percent Sunni. The Sunnis do not have one

religious leader. Instead, they have distinguished scholars and jurists who issue opinions. The Shiites glorify Ali (circa A.D. 599–661), the prophet Muhammad's son-in-law and cousin, as Muhammad's only successor and believe all future successors should come through his line. Sunnis and Shiites also observe differences in their methods of worship. In general, Sunnis in Iraq are wealthier than Kurds or Shiites and observe a less strict form of Islam in their daily lives.

Modern Iraq has a young population, with almost 40 percent fourteen years old or younger. Only 3 percent are aged sixty-five or older. The literacy rate among Iraqis has fluctuated depending on government policy. In modern Iraq, an estimated 40 percent of citizens over the age of fifteen can read and write.

Throughout history, the people living along the Tigris and Euphrates rivers have primarily made their living through agriculture.

In the north, agriculture relied on highland rainfall. In the arid south, it depended on irrigation and flood control. Seasonal flooding in the south takes place before most crops have ripened. Consequently, floodwaters must be controlled by a network of dikes (walls) and canals. Salination from nearby Gulf waters is a constant problem. Aging desalination and drainage systems must be updated and maintained to prevent floodwater and irrigation water from damaging the fields.

Between 1947 and 1980, Iraq experienced a massive change in population as people left the countryside to live in the cities. Poor people flocked to the cities to earn more money. By 1980 an estimated 69 percent of the nation's population lived in urban areas and 31 percent in rural areas. Baghdad attracted the most people. By 2005 about one-fourth of Iraq's people lived in the capital, making it the country's largest city, with a population of nearly seven million. Basra and Mosul each had more than a million people, and Kirkuk more than six hundred thousand.

THE ECONOMY

Oil completely dominates Iraq's economy. The U.S. Energy Information Administration estimates that Iraq has the world's second-largest proven reserves of oil. Iraq also contains a huge amount of natural gas. The expanding worldwide demand for oil was a boon for Iraq's economy. By 1989 oil contributed 61 percent of Iraq's gross domestic product (GDP, the value of goods and services produced in a country in a year). Until the Gulf War in 1991, oil exports brought in about 95 percent of Iraq's foreign exchange. In the years between the Gulf War and the Iraq War, production and exports fell sharply. Oil production has approached pre-Gulf War levels since the U.S.-led coalition forces occupation of Iraq but is still at less than half its potential, due to an aging infrastructure.

By the early 1980s, Iraq had almost reached the standards of developed countries in the areas of health care and education. Iraq possessed a modern telecommunications network, a reliable electricity grid, and sophisticated water treatment facilities that provided potable (drinkable) water for most of the population. However, when Saddam Hussein took control of Iraq's government in 1979, Iraq's ability to profit from its oil wealth became limited by almost constant war and deep corruption.

Iraq's proven oil reserve holds more than 112 billion barrels of oil. The entire Persian Gulf has a proven oil reserve of 715 billion barrels. Iraq also has an estimated 110 trillion cubic feet (3 trillion cubic m) of natural gas. The United States consumes more than 7 billion barrels a year, while the entire world uses more than 30 billion.

Except for oil, Iraq never had a large industrial sector. Within the industrial sector, the petroleum industry is by far the most important. Other industries include chemicals, textiles, leather, construction materials, food processing, fertilizer, and metal fabrication/processing.

In modern Iraq, agriculture remains the largest source of economic activity but not economic wealth. About 13 percent of the land is arable. Until the war with Iran began in 1980, Iraq was the world's largest date producer. Other major crops include grains, lentils and beans, rice, cotton, and sesame. Farmers also raise livestock including cattle, sheep, and poultry. The economic sanctions of the 1990s led to a decline in production, and it dropped even

IRAQI WOMEN HARVEST DATES IN A DATE PALM TREE FIELD SOUTH OF
Baghdad in 2002.

further during the war of the early 2000s. As of 2008, U.S.-sponsored aid programs had been established to restore agricultural productivity to Iraq.

LIVING IN WARTIME

During his rule, Saddam Hussein initiated two foreign wars (the Iran–Iraq War and the Gulf War) and provoked a third (the Iraq War, starting in 2003). The Iraqi people have had to adjust to living in wartime and postwar conditions. They have become expert at fixing, patching, and recycling everyday items, such as worn tires—or simply doing without.

The Iran–Iraq War lasted nearly eight years. During that time, it dominated Iraqi life. In order to maintain civilian morale in the face of a war going poorly, Saddam continued to pursue ambitious economic development projects. He paid for them by spending his nation's cash and by obtaining money from foreign countries including Saudi Arabia and Kuwait. Baghdad experienced major new construction projects. Nationwide, public spending rose from $21 billion in 1980 to $29.5 billion in 1982. Most of this was for civilian imports of everyday items so that Iraqi citizens would not experience consumer shortages. Saddam wanted life to appear as normal as possible for as many people as possible.

In order to maintain military morale, Saddam provided monetary rewards. Families who lost a son or father in war received thirty thousand dollars. Officers who displayed heroism received Rolex watches with Saddam's face on the dial. Veterans received preferential treatment when cars and houses were available for purchase.

Families who had lost a child received a free car, a free plot of land, or a free loan to build a house.

Saddam also gave the family of each dead soldier a Toyota car. Citizens began to sing a well-known Iraqi children's tune after adding new lyrics:

Now my father will return from the front
Nailed to his coffin
My mother will marry another man,
But I will ride a new Toyota.

The pretense that everything during wartime was going well could not be maintained, however. By the summer of 1982, Iraq began to experience serious financial problems because the war with Iran had interfered with its ability to export oil. Civilian imports declined dramatically, and consumers began to experience shortages. Government spending also declined. The government stopped paying families who lost a member in the war.

Saddam called on Iraqi citizens to sacrifice for the cause. The call was both an appeal to patriotism and a threat. Peasants donated their life savings. The rich gave gold and jewels. Soldiers went door-to-door asking for donations. At night announcers on Iraqi television read a long list of worthy people and how much they had contributed. Saddam spoke on TV one evening about a millionaire from his hometown of Tikrit who had given a mere three thousand dollars. Saddam sarcastically asked, "How much faith does this man have in the homeland and the revolution?" The president added ominously, "I'm sure he will hear me."

Nonetheless, Saddam correctly sensed that the economic downturn was causing his popularity to decline. He responded by further tightening control over all aspects of the country. His security forces expanded until they numbered an estimated 208,000, about 15 percent of all government workers.

ARTISTS AND FILMMAKERS

Saddam had a high regard for people with artistic skills. For this reason, actors and playwrights enjoyed a privileged position, as long as they promoted Baathist goals. The Ministry of Culture produced propaganda films during the Iran–Iraq War. After the Gulf War, Iraq produced a film about Iraqi efforts to drive out the British during the 1930s. The purpose of the film was to advance the idea that Kuwait was a rightful province of Iraq. In addition to military propaganda films, the government sponsored films that praised the virtues of the working class. During the 1970s and 1980s, the government sponsored films that praised the labors of poor farmers. Such films were in keeping with the Baath Party's Socialist roots. During the 1990s, the subject changed to so-called documentaries depicting brave citizens struggling against international economic sanctions.

Because the Iraqi film and television industry was small, many actors and actresses who graduated from the Iraqi Academy of Fine Arts turned to local theater. There they performed short skits poking fun at acceptable targets, such as rural Shiites who moved to the big cities. But these skits also explored some social issues, such as the rise of organized crime gangs and the collapse of family values under the economic stresses imposed by international sanctions.

Even while the Iraqi military and civilians suffered, Saddam made sure that members of his family grew rich. Saddam's extended family, including his sons, in-laws, and cousins, controlled state-run industries. Stories spread throughout Iraq about the Hussein family's extravagant lifestyle. Adnan Khairallah,

ALI HASSAN AL-MAJID'S VERSION OF JUSTICE

In 1984 one of Saddam's cousins, Ali Hassan al-Majid, was director general of the Iraqi secret police. Upon assuming command of the secret police, Ali conducted a meeting with other high-ranking government officials. He proudly announced the beginning of a new policy: "Before I came into this office, wrongdoers in this nation simply disappeared. They would be given a prison sentence, or even executed, but the family would not be notified where they were or how much time they would have to serve for their crime . . . or even if they were alive. This was wrong. . . . From this time on, when a criminal is arrested, charged and sentenced, families will be notified. Perhaps the family will choose to disown these traitors."

Ali demonstrated how this new policy would work. He summoned a man to the stage. The man said that his son had been arrested six months earlier and he did not know what had become of him. Ali sorted through some papers, pulled out a cassette tape, and replied, "Your son was accused of high treason. He has been executed. . . . Here is a tape of his confession."

The father was overcome with shock and sorrow. Ali smiled broadly and loudly proclaimed to the audience, "It is good for that father to know his son is a traitor."

Saddam's brother-in-law and Iraq's defense minister, collected a large fleet of expensive cars. Saddam's sons, Uday and Qusay, did the same. Iraq's citizens recognized that the greed and corruption of the Hussein family knew few bounds, but they felt powerless to stop it.

For the next six hours, person after person presented Ali with the name of a relative who was missing. In most cases, Ali happily provided the answer that the arrested person had been executed. Then he summoned a tall man dressed in rags. His skin looked like burnt toast. His hair had melted into his skull. His open mouth revealed no teeth. His fingers were torn and clotted with blood. The man explained that he had been tortured, his teeth removed with pliers, and his nails ripped from his hands and feet. Finally, he was placed in an oven and slowly roasted. All of this stemmed from a letter his wife sent to the secret police. His wife claimed that he was an enemy of the state.

Ali summoned the wife. He told the audience that this woman was of Iranian descent and that while her husband was in the army, she had turned her home into a house of prostitution. When the husband returned from the front, she allegedly tried to protect herself from him by denouncing him to the secret police. Only after the husband's arrest, interrogation, and punishment did the supposed truth come out. Now Ali wanted to deliver his version of justice. The woman and her children were to be dumped between the lines of the Iraqi and Iranian armies. There the artillery shells would fall so thick that they would be killed.

Ali laughed and concluded, "I am a kind man. I am a good man. I seek justice. . . ." He continued laughing while the audience applauded.

Corruption trickled down to the lower ranks, as well. Saddam's security forces received cash bonuses for each arrest they made. Then the agents routinely extorted (obtained by force or intimidation) money from the families of the prisoners. They said that the prisoner would receive more lenient treatment based on the amount of money the family provided. Richer citizens sold their homes and cars to raise the money. Poorer people sold whatever they owned.

In 1986 came a warning for anyone considering criticizing Saddam and his henchmen. Saddam signed a decree that read:

Anyone insulting publicly in any way the President of the Republic, or his office, or the Revolutionary Command Council, or the Arab Baath Socialist Party, or the Government, is punishable by life imprisonment. . . . The punishment will be execution if the insult or attack is done in a blatant fashion.

The government worked hard to control the public mood. As Iraqi casualties mounted in the Iran–Iraq War, the government began to discourage traditional public displays of grief and mourning. It forbade elaborate funerals. The only public place where a family could mourn the loss of a son was within a mosque. An American reporter described the scene inside: "The calm rhetoric and vows to die for Saddam did not exist. Women, most of them mothers, touched and kissed the holy shrine and wailed, over and over, 'Oh God, Oh God, please make this war end. We have lost our sons. We have lost our brothers.' "

Nearly twenty years later, a woman recalled her childhood in Baghdad during the Iran–Iraq War: "The big cities felt like a military base. Every other car was a military car, with soldiers coming and going all the time. As kids, my brother and I used to wave at passing military cars with young soldiers in the back. We would flash them with victory signs, but they would shake their fingers at us and make an upside down V—the opposite of victory. The soldiers were so bitter; their life was gone."

As economic conditions worsened and the Iran–Iraq War continued to take away the men, many women turned to prostitution in order to earn enough money to feed their children. They could earn more money in neighboring countries, so they began slipping over the border. Saddam learned of this and issued a new law making it illegal for women to travel alone. They could travel only in the presence of a husband or a male relative to whom they could not be married, such as a brother. Agents arrested, imprisoned, and tortured many women who violated this law.

ANOTHER WAR LOOMS

Once the war with Iran ended, Iraqis hoped for a return to normalcy. International sanctions had severely limited imports. The lifting of those sanctions hinted at better times ahead. Instead came the 1990 Iraqi invasion of Kuwait and the ensuing confrontation with the U.S.-led coalition forces. Iraqis were worried, frustrated, and uncertain about the future.

Immediately after Iraq's invasion of Kuwait, the Iraqi people rejoiced over their conquest. Historically, Kuwait had been ruled from Iraq. Saddam and leaders before him described Kuwait as the nineteenth province of Iraq. In addition, instant economic benefits flowed from the invasion. The Iraqi military looted Kuwait and sent much of the booty back home. Suddenly Baghdad commuters could step aboard shiny new Mercedes buses taken from Kuwait. Shoppers found the shops and markets full of looted consumer items: Rolex watches, British chocolates, Italian designer clothing, and Japanese electronics.

However, civilian enthusiasm for the invasion waned when people began to realize that most of the world condemned the Iraqi invasion. The UN economic embargo took effect, and the supply of consumer goods diminished. In September 1990, the government imposed rationing. In December Baghdad radio summoned all healthy males born in 1957 to report for military duty. It was a shock for thirty-three-year-old men to have to return to the military since most had already served for at least eight years during the Iran–Iraq War.

As the coalition forces began to mass along Iraq's borders, civilians realized that another war was imminent. The wealthy fled Baghdad. Those who remained and had enough money stockpiled food and water. Most people experienced severe food shortages. Their food rationing coupons became less valuable as the price of scarce foods soared. The citizens of Baghdad lined up for hours simply to buy staples such as bread. One by one, restaurants and hotels began to run out of food.

The economic embargo caused factories to close because they could not obtain the resources to continue to function. Spare parts were in such short supply that vehicles could no longer run. The price of two automobile tires soared 700 percent between the summer of 1989 and year's end. Crime increased, which was particularly shocking since in the past the security forces had maintained law and order. Before, the security forces had swept beggars off the streets. Now they reappeared, but the security forces did nothing.

It was clear that government authorities were losing their grip on day-to-day control of the population.

No people in history had experienced an air assault like that delivered by the coalition forces beginning on January 17, 1991. Bombs and missiles rained down for about five weeks. Their purpose was to demoralize the Iraqis and weaken their will to resist the coming invasion. Iraqi civilians, particularly those living in Baghdad, could do little but huddle in their bomb shelters. Occasionally, the coalition air forces mistakenly attacked the wrong target. Such was the case on February 13, 1991, when bombs destroyed a bunker complex thought to be sheltering high-ranking Baathist leaders. About three hundred civilians were killed.

After three weeks of aerial attack, major cities had neither electricity nor running water because power plants had been bombed.

BOMBS AND MISSILES COLOR THE NIGHT SKY OVER BAGHDAD DURING A
coalition air strike in early 1991.

The government announced an indefinite ban on the sale of fuel. Civilian vehicle traffic came to a stop.

Because displays of wealth attracted attention from the Baath Party, which might devise ways to confiscate people's riches, even wealthy businessmen tried to appear poor. As one reported, "If you have the money for a Mercedes, don't buy one. You cannot dare to show yourself." Businessmen also learned that making long-term plans made little sense because unexpected events happened regularly: "One morning you wake up and everything has changed: the dinar [the Iraqi currency] collapsed, Saddam invaded Kuwait, your uncle was thrown in jail."

When the Gulf War ended, Iraqis continued to suffer because of the UN-imposed trade embargo. Iraq could not sell its oil, so the country had little ability to purchase imports. Also, as part of the UN effort aimed at destroying Iraq's WMD programs, dual-use items (products that had legitimate uses, but could also be used to create WMD) were blocked from entering Iraq. UN authorities worried that Iraqi technicians could use these items—which included pesticides, fertilizers, industrial chemicals, and agricultural machines such as crop dusters—to manufacture WMD and their delivery systems. So they prevented Iraq from importing these items. However, this prohibition kept Iraqi farmers and factory workers from making legitimate use of these vital items.

The already weakened economy declined even more as agricultural and industrial production collapsed and inflation soared. Iraq's electrical grid went unrepaired. Its water purification system collapsed. In 1992 the price of food climbed 2,000 percent compared to prices before Saddam ordered the invasion of Kuwait. The poor went hungry. The middle class eked out a bleak existence. Waterborne diseases including typhoid and cholera spread. Disease and malnutrition caused the infant mortality rate to soar. UN experts estimated that in 1993 about eighty thousand to one hundred thousand children died because of the impact of UN economic sanctions.

During most of the 1990s, the Iraqi people suffered from the economic sanctions. A middle-class resident of Baghdad recalled that before the 1990s, "We lived well off subsidies [payments] from an oil-rich government. But with inflation and sanctions, we were suddenly faced with pressing daily needs." Importers stockpiled goods in neighboring countries and paid men to smuggle the goods into Iraq. Soon organized bands of criminals became involved. The most skilled smugglers and gangsters made exorbitant profits. Iraqis coined

WOMEN SELL COOKING OIL AND food at a market in Baghdad in 1996. Economic sanctions made basic supplies expensive.

a new word to describe them: *Qitat al-Hisar* (cats of the embargo).

Saddam exploited his citizens' suffering to influence Western public opinion to abandon the sanctions. Once the sanctions were lifted and the UN inspectors left Iraq, Saddam again took steps to ease the lives of his people. Damage from the coalition bombing during the Gulf War was repaired. Electrical service returned to normal levels. Medicines became widely available. Growing prosperity meant that trendy shops catering to the wealthy again filled with the latest European fashions, while markets in the poorer districts stocked food and cheap Chinese-manufactured electronics.

Public construction projects provided jobs. Many of these projects glorified Saddam and his achievements. One of the largest was the Umm al-Maarik (Mother of All Battles) mosque built in central Baghdad. Completed in 2002, it celebrated Iraq's supposed victory against the coalition in 1991.

SADDAM BUILT THE UMM AL-MAARIK MOSQUE *(ABOVE)* ON THE OUTSKIRTS of Baghdad to honor his achievements in the 1991 war against the coalition. The minarets (columns) that surround the mosque are designed to look like Scud missiles, and the mosque houses a 605-page Quran written in Saddam's blood.

EDUCATION

The literacy rate for people over the age of five was just 11 percent in 1947. The government mandated compulsory education in 1958, but the campaign was not fully implemented until the 1970s. In 1978 the Baath Party launched the Comprehensive National Campaign for the Compulsory Eradication of Illiteracy. The campaign's overt goal was to teach reading and writing to the poor, both male and female. The government claimed that it raised the national literacy rate from 42 percent in 1975 to 87 percent in 1985. The literacy campaign so impressed the UN that from 1980 to 1991 it granted awards to individual Iraqis and various Iraqi educational organizations. Frequent war and the collapse of the Iraqi economy under the weight of international sanctions, however, caused the education system to erode. Further adding to the failure of the education system was the Baath Party's emphasis on political goals to the exclusion of basic education.

As early as 1973, Saddam told a committee charged with designing a new educational curriculum what he wanted: "In order to perform your duties correctly, you must be precisely aware of our central concepts, both ideological and political." The most important "central concept" was that the Baath Party was all important: "This party leads the community not only in accordance with its own values, organization and ideology but also in accordance with its own policies." Quite simply, Saddam and other party leaders wanted the education system to play a leading role in creating a new generation of Baathists.

Later, as Saddam became dictator, education became even more politicized. Teachers rewarded students for such accomplishments as informing on their family or memorizing Saddam's sayings. Consequently, by 1995 the literacy rate fell to 45 percent.

From grade school on, students memorized Baathist slogans and songs. One such slogan related to a tyrant who ruled part of Iraq during the time of Ottoman control. The tyrant, a governor named Hajjaj, had ruled with an iron fist. The Baath Party celebrated his rule by requiring Iraqi ninth graders to memorize one of his sayings: "I see heads that are ripe, and I am the one to pluck them. . . . O people of Iraq, people of discord and deceit . . . I will bind you like a bundle of twigs. I will beat you like stray camels."

The Baath Party tried to sever the bond between parents and children. It wanted to replace parental authority with party authority. To accomplish this goal, teachers encouraged children to inform on the parents. A teacher's guide published in 1977 told teachers: "Teach the student to object to his parents if he hears them discussing state secrets. . . . You must place in every corner a son of the revolution, with a trustworthy eye and a firm mind."

Baath Party recruits who excelled in high school or had the right political connections received a place in a public university.

Such a position was particularly welcome because a university student could avoid the military draft. If a potential university student lacked connections with the Baath Party, his or her only hope to gain admittance was to have a wealthy parent who could afford to pay tuition in a private college.

Students selected for possible admission into the Baath Party received special treatment at school. Once a week, they wore a green Baath Party uniform to school. They helped plan celebrations honoring Saddam. These celebrations occurred on special days, such as Saddam's birthday or the day that commemorates the Baath Party's rise to power. Teachers observed the behavior of their students and reported promising students to Baath Party recruiters. The recruiters rewarded such students by taking them on field trips to visit military camps.

A student who fled from Iraq recalled his experience with the Baath Party: "I was only sixteen at the time and in high school but [party officials] kept coming around to me and insisting that I join the party. They tried to sign everybody up, and those who did join were then forced to become informers. I told them I wasn't interested in politics, I just wanted to concentrate on my studies, but they wouldn't take no for an answer."

WOMEN'S RIGHTS

An act passed by the Revolutionary Command Council on December 19, 1972, defined the main functions of the Federation of Iraqi Women: "to mobilize Iraqi women to fight against imperialism, Zionism [modern Israel], reactionary trends, and backwardness."

The need to liberate women was a central part of the Baath Party strategy to develop Iraq. At the same time, Saddam and other party leaders retained the traditional view that a woman's role as a mother was a crucial part of her social and political responsibilities.

Still, women in Iraq enjoyed more legal and economic freedom than in almost any other Muslim country. They could dress in Western-style clothing, attend college, vote, and drive cars. According to Iraqi government statistics, during the 1980s women provided "46% of all teachers, 29% of physicians, 46% of dentists, 70% of pharmacists, 15% of factory workers, and 16% of governmental employees."

IRAQI WOMEN ATTEND A CLASS AT al-Mustansiriya University in Baghdad in the early 1990s.

The decade of the 1970s witnessed some legal changes benefiting Iraqi women. Judges could overturn a father's wish for his daughter to marry at a young age. Forced marriages were declared illegal, and the minimum age of marriage was increased to eighteen. The armed forces began admitting women. On the other hand, women still could not obtain divorces, but men could. Polygamy, in which a husband has more than one wife at the same time, was still lawful, as long as the first wife agreed. Given that Iraqi men continued to dominate Iraqi women, such agreement seldom reflected what a wife really wanted. Overall, though, the 1970s and 1980s saw a considerable rise in Iraqi standards of living due to Iraq's booming oil sales, and women, as well as men, benefited.

The 1990s, with the Gulf War and subsequent international economic sanctions, changed life in Iraq. The economic sanctions struck women particularly hard. The sanctions caused widespread unemployment, particularly within the public sector, the largest employer of women. Uncontrolled inflation reduced buying power. According to a report on women in Iraq, "The salaries of schoolteachers, doctors, social workers, engineers and technicians became almost worthless. Young women in the big cities, who had enjoyed financial independence with a salary of around $400 a month a few years earlier, suddenly found that their real wages were reduced to less than $2 a month."

During the Iraq War of the early 2000s, women's rights are not a high priority for the Iraqi government because of the unstable conditions that exist in Iraq. There has also been a resurgence of traditional Islamic law in some areas of the country. A strict, traditional interpretation of Islamic law does not advance rights for women that are equal to those of men.

CHAPTER 9

THE IRAQ

BY THE TIME SADDAM ENTERED HIS SIXTIES, he was not the man he had once been. Fear of assassination kept him from mingling with the Iraqi people as he had done in the past. Indeed, he did not even attend his own sixty-fifth birthday party on April 28, 2002, even though it was held in his tribal stronghold of Tikrit. He continued to change residences every few days to foil potential assassins. Because he was afraid of being poisoned, he had all his food examined by a team of nuclear scientists before he ate it.

He remained personally vain, dyeing his hair and mustache to hide the gray and swimming every day to retain his physique. Because he walked with a slight limp, he would not allow himself to be filmed walking. He required reading glasses but would not allow anyone to film him wearing them.

His isolation and constant movement seemed to make him

detached from reality. Whereas in the past he could efficiently manage a political or military meeting, he seemed increasingly unable to do so. Meetings lasted for hours without reaching decisions. He often concluded meetings by telling his staff that they might not see him for a while because he was too busy.

THE WAR ON TERROR

Meanwhile, in the wake of the September 11, 2001, al-Qaeda terror attacks against the United States, President George W. Bush changed U.S. policy toward Iraq. In his State of the Union address of January 2002, Bush announced that his war on terror would include countries that provided shelter for terrorists and that developed weapons of mass destruction. The Bush administration had concluded that Iraq was one of these countries.

Saddam responded to mounting American and British pressure to submit to weapons inspections just as he had always done. He looked for ways to exploit divisions among his potential foes. Russia, France, and Germany—traditionally allies of the United States and Great Britain—all had benefited economically from trade with Iraq. Saddam worked to strengthen his ties with these trading partners. He thought that they would block international action, especially that led by the United States and Britain, against his regime.

He blustered and threatened. In a televised address to the Iraqi people on January 17, 2002 (the anniversary of the start of the Gulf War), Saddam said: "Today is a day in the Grand Battle, the immortal Mother of All Battles. It is a glorious and a splendid day on the part of the self-respecting people of Iraq and their history, and it is the beginning of the great shame for those who ignited its fire on the other part. It is the first day on which the vast military phase of that battle started. Or rather, it is the first day of that battle, since Allah decreed that the Mother of All Battles continue till this day."

On October 15, 2002, the Baath Party held a presidential election. Saddam was the only candidate on the ballot. Saddam's campaign theme song was "I Will Always Love You," a hit song by American pop singer Whitney Houston. The song was played repeatedly on Iraqi radio and television. The campaign motto was "Everyone loves Saddam." According to official Iraqi sources, every eligible voter in Iraq voted and Saddam won 100 percent of the vote.

Saddam failed to appreciate fully the concerns of Western governments over his WMD program. Because of these concerns, the UN passed Resolution 1441 on November 8, 2002. The resolution deplored "the fact that Iraq has not provided an accurate, full, final, and complete disclosure of all aspects of its . . . programmes to develop weapons of mass destruction and ballistic missiles." It called for a new round of inspections, "an enhanced inspection regime with the aim of bringing to full and verified completion the disarmament process" inside Iraq. It provided a tight timetable for Iraq to accept the demands of the resolution. Lastly, it warned that there would be "serious consequences" if Iraq failed to comply.

IRAQIS CELEBRATE THE REELECTION of Saddam in October 2002. Most Western leaders believed the vote and subsequent celebrations were orchestrated by Saddam's government.

Saddam responded to the resolution with his usual tactics. He tried to divide the members of the UN Security Council. He sought to gain time by accepting parts of the resolution. He also made speeches on Iraqi television warning his people to prepare for their third war of his twenty-three-year reign. In an effort to make himself more popular, he ordered the mass release of prisoners from the notorious Abu Ghraib prison. What the public did not know was that, before releasing the common criminals, he had ordered the execution of all remaining political prisoners.

UN INSPECTION

Saddam finally agreed to the UN demands, and UN inspectors entered Iraq on November 27, 2002, after a nearly four-year absence. Saddam instructed his officials to appear to cooperate with the inspectors. He placed his trust in the elaborate measures undertaken to conceal his WMD program, which included research and development. In addition, Saddam was confident that his scientists would not talk candidly to UN inspectors because they feared the consequences. Saddam's deceptions mostly worked. As one official reported, "The Iraqis were much better at concealment than we thought they were going to be."

To the frustration of the Bush administration, the UN inspectors reported that Iraq was complying with Resolution 1441. However, American and British intelligence experts discovered that the Iraqis had failed to provide a full accounting of their WMD activities. On December 19, 2002, President Bush declared that Iraq was in breach of (not totally following) the UN resolution.

In Iraq, people began to understand that another war was likely. The government provided extra food so people could stockpile supplies. Saddam gave a December 25, 2002, speech in which he called for the people to be ready to sacrifice their lives for the nation. Saddam and his trusted lieutenants prepared the military for war.

Saddam hoped that his forces could inflict enough losses on U.S. troops so the United States would give up. He believed that the United States' recent record showed that it lacked the resolve for a tough fight. After all, he reasoned, in 1993, the Americans departed Somalia after losing just eighteen soldiers in a battle in the African nation's capital, Mogadishu. Likewise, the terrorist bombing of the

U.S. Marine Corps barracks in Beirut, Lebanon, on October 23, 1983, had killed several hundred marines and sent the Americans home. And the Vietnam War, in which the United States participated from 1965 to 1975, was another example of American inability to fight a long, tough war.

Many people around the globe believed that war with Iraq was unnecessary. The leaders of Germany, France, Russia, and China favored disarming Saddam by peaceful measures. These countries were the same ones that benefited economically by working with Saddam's regime. Many leaders doubted the existence of a solid WMD program in Iraq since evidence was contradictory and difficult to prove. Yet Saddam failed to deter President Bush and his main ally British prime minister Tony Blair. These two leaders were convinced that Saddam's alleged stockpile of WMD and his regime's support of terrorists against his own people presented mortal peril to freedom-loving people. They worked to assemble a military alliance to confront Saddam.

On March 17, 2003, President George W. Bush made the highly controversial case for war against Iraq. His most pressing arguments in support of war included:

FRENCH PRESIDENT JACQUES Chirac *(left)* **and German leader Gerhard Schroeder meet in 2003 to discuss their appeal to the United States to find a peaceful solution to the Iraq crisis.**

Intelligence gathered by this and other governments leaves

voices in the wilderness uk

WAR KILLS THE ...QI LIVES

INNOCENT

DON'T ATTACK IRAQ

IN THE FIRING LINE
NO WAR ON IRAQ

PROTESTERS AGAINST THE invasion of Iraq gather outside a British military building near London in early 2003.

no doubt that the Iraq regime continues to possess and conceal some of the most lethal weapons ever devised. This regime has already used weapons of mass destruction against Iraq's neighbors and against Iraq's people. . . .

The danger is clear: using chemical, biological or, one day, nuclear weapons, obtained with the help of Iraq, the terrorists could fulfill their stated ambitions and kill thousands or hundreds of thousands of innocent people in our country, or any other. . . .

The security of the world requires disarming Saddam Hussein now.

President Bush gave Saddam and his sons forty-eight hours to leave Iraq. When Saddam finally realized that war was imminent, he sent his wives and daughters out of the country for safety. Then he made his final preparations.

Saddam was a poor military leader. Even though he possessed no formal military training, he had tried to direct all military operations. He had done this twice before, against Iran and when he invaded Kuwait. It had not worked then and worked even less well the third time. His unwillingness to delegate authority had seriously hampered his generals. They could not react quickly to changing battlefield conditions. Instead, they were afraid to do anything until they received orders from Saddam

WAR WITH IRAQ

On March 19, 2003, in the face of widespread international opposition, the war against Iraq began as U.S.-led coalition planes and missiles attacked military targets in Iraq. Iraqi command and control centers were particular targets. Most especially, the coalition tried to find and kill Saddam. The next day, coalition ground forces entered Iraq. U.S. forces rapidly advanced toward Baghdad. On April 1, a Baath Party official read a speech written by Saddam that urged the Iraqi people to fight hard: "They are aggressors, evil, accursed by God. . . . You shall be victorious and they shall be vanquished."

On April 7, U.S. forces entered Baghdad. That same day, a U.S. missile narrowly missed killing Saddam. Saddam made a decision. He would no longer act as head of state. Instead, he became a fugitive. Saddam spent the last days of his rule hoping that his guerrilla forces, the Fedayeen, would tie down U.S. forces and cause them to lose heart. He spent considerable time composing handwritten notes to his lieutenants full of instructions about how to wage the fight. He had to use written instructions because he correctly feared that the allies would find him if he used a radio or cell phone.

Saddam made his last public appearance at the Adhimya mosque in a Baghdad suburb on April 9, 2003. Then, without telling anyone about his plans, he fled. He had arranged many safe houses (places where a person can take refuge or engage in secret activities) throughout the country. He moved from one to another in a dilapidated taxi so as not to attract attention. U.S. forces relentlessly pursued him.

Saddam spent the next eight months as a fugitive. He moved from safe house to safe house while a small network of family and clan provided security, food, clothing, and supplies. He had regular meetings with his sons Uday and Qusay. At these meetings, Saddam plotted strategy for his return to power. It was not to be.

On July 21, 2003, the Americans found and killed Uday and Qusay in the northern city of Mosul. Most Iraqis rejoiced when they learned the news that these ruthless, torturous sons of Saddam were dead. On December 13, U.S. forces acted on an intelligence tip obtained from one of Saddam's former bodyguards. He said that Saddam could be found at the village of al-Dawr, about 8 miles (13 km) south of Tikrit. This was near the place where Saddam had claimed he had swum across the Tigris River while fleeing authorities back in 1959.

American Special Forces and soldiers from the U.S. 4th Infantry moved through orange groves and sunflower fields toward a farmhouse. Two armed men ran from one of the buildings. The Americans quickly overpowered and captured them. The Americans surrounded the one-story farm hut and moved in. They found a filthy bedroom with a bare mattress. On top of the mattress was a pile of T-shirts and socks, still in their plastic wrappings, suggesting fresh clothes for a fugitive on the run. When they found a green metal suitcase packed with $750,000, they knew Saddam was nearby.

Outside, soldiers discovered a trapdoor covered with a carpet. They lifted the door to reveal an 8-foot-deep (2.4 m) hole just large enough to shelter a single man. They dragged out an aged man

CELEBRATING THE CAPTURE OF SADDAM

The capture of Saddam Hussein on December 13, 2003, was the cause for celebration around the world. The first to celebrate were the U.S. soldiers who captured him. A reporter observed their return from a nighttime mission. He didn't know what had happened, but he saw the returning soldiers talking excitedly and taking pictures of one another.

When the news of Saddam's capture became public, Iraqis danced in the streets of Baghdad, although no public celebration took place in the streets of Saddam's hometown of Tikrit. At the news conference announcing the capture, Iraqi journalists viewed a video of the captive Saddam and erupted into cheers and chants of "Death to Saddam!"

with wild, unkempt hair and a straggly beard flecked with gray. The man said, "I am Saddam Hussein. I am president of Iraq and I am ready to negotiate." A U.S. soldier replied, "President Bush sends his regards."

TRIAL AND EXECUTION

The U.S. military held the former dictator in a specially constructed detention center near Baghdad Airport. A former Iraqi official visited him and asked why he had killed so many people during his twenty-three-year reign. Saddam answered that they were all "thieves and Iranian spies." The official said that Saddam "seemed rather tired and haggard, but he was unrepentant and defiant."

A team from the U.S. Central Intelligence Agency interrogated Saddam at length. The CIA particularly wanted to know about Saddam's WMD programs and about his alleged link with the al-Qaeda terrorist group. The interrogations were unproductive. In the early spring of 2004, the CIA gave up. The Federal Bureau of Investigation (FBI) took over interrogations. The FBI's goal was to obtain evidence for use in trying Saddam for war crimes.

In July the Americans handed over Saddam and other captured Baathist figures to the Iraqi government. However, U.S. soldiers continued to provide prison security. Saddam was kept in solitary confinement except when he appeared before Iraq's Special Tribunal, consisting of five Iraqi judges. The tribunal was charged with investigating, prosecuting, and trying Saddam. According to Iraqi law, no jury trial would take place. The trial marked a historic first. Never before had a member state of the United Nations chosen, on its own, to bring a former leader "before a national court to try him for crimes recognized under international law."

This tribunal met in one of Saddam's former palaces on the outskirts of Baghdad. When the tribunal's judge asked Saddam's name, he replied, "I am the president of Iraq." This proved to be Saddam's main line of defense during his subsequent trial. Regardless of the evidence brought before the court, Saddam said that he was the legitimate ruler of the country and that the court did not have the legal right to try him.

On October 19, 2005, the first criminal trial of the Special Tribunal met. The prosecution confronted Saddam and seven other defendants. The prosecution's case centered on the al-Dujail massacre, which had taken place in 1982. Prosecutors alleged that Saddam's security forces detained 687 persons and executed more than 100 people. The prosecution alleged that a total of 399 women, children, and elderly men were sent to a desert prison. It also alleged that another 46 people were tortured to death in prison.

By Western standards, the lack of a jury of Saddam's peers to decide his fate made the trial unfair. Human Rights Watch, an organization that had been a constant Saddam critic, sharply criticized the trial. Still, Saddam enjoyed certain rights never given to people arrested by his own security services. Saddam and the other defendants heard the charges against them in person. They had defense lawyers and the right to call witnesses.

SADDAM LISTENS WHILE THE prosecution presents its case against him during his trial in Baghdad in 2006.

In its closing argument on June 19, 2006, the prosecution demanded the death penalty for Saddam and three of his codefendants. Saddam was found guilty, and on November 5, 2006, he was sentenced to death by hanging. The sentence was carried out on December 30, 2006. A video of the execution appeared on the Internet. It showed Shiite prison guards mocking Saddam as he prayed in the moments before his death. Saddam's half brother, Barzan Hassan, who was the former intelligence chief, and Awad Bandar, former head of Iraq's Revolutionary Court, were hanged on January 15, 2007, for their parts in the al-Dujail massacre. Taha Ramadan, Saddam's former deputy and vice president, was executed by hanging on March 20, 2007.

IRAQ

THE BAATH PARTY HAD CONTROLLED IRAQ FOR THIRTY-FIVE YEARS.

The overthrow of Saddam Hussein liberated the country from Baath tyranny and brutal dictatorship. With the exception of the Sunni elite who had benefited from Saddam's rule, most Iraqis were glad to see the change. A survey in March 2004 found that 56 percent of the people thought that Saddam's removal had improved their lives. This figure also meant that a large number of people thought that they were less well off than before. Furthermore, as time passed, attitudes changed with the ebb and flow of violence and disorder. Despite the transfer of power from the coalition forces to an Iraqi government in June 2004, insurgents continued to disrupt Iraqi society with murders, bombings, suicide attacks, threats, and intimidation. Insurgent groups included Baathists and Islamic extremists, as well as Shiite militia. Nonetheless, in the face of threats of violence, more than half

AFTER SADDAM

of all Iraqi voters demonstrated their commitment to democratic change by turning out to vote for legislators in January 2005.

Some of the popular discontent stemmed from the slow pace of recovery after Saddam's removal from power. At first, the new Iraqi government and the United States were unable to provide many basic services, such as reliable electricity. Yet Iraqis had made do with unreliable electricity during each of Saddam's three wars. Popular discontent had a deeper cause. Iraqis were a proud people. They were humiliated by the ease with which the coalition powers had overrun their country. Worse, from their perspective, they had to live under foreign occupation. Moreover, as time passed, neither their own government nor the U.S. forces were able to provide consistent security against insurgents. The increase in U.S. military forces that began in January 2007, however, brought a dramatic decrease in the number of attacks by insurgents. How enduring this decrease will be is yet to be determined.

The United States also made several policy blunders that contributed to popular discontent. Some of the mistakes were understandable. For example, the United States promoted a "debaathification" program. It was designed to remove Baathist influence in the civil service and in the military. Consequently, more than five hundred thousand Iraqis lost their jobs. While this number included some hard-core Baathists, it also included many more who had simply joined the Baath Party because they wanted to provide for their families. The debaathification program created economic and administrative turmoil. It angered many Iraqis and helped create a volatile environment for exploitation by insurgents.

Another important mistake committed by U.S. leaders involved the demobilization (disbanding; discharging from military service) of the Iraqi army. As soon as U.S. forces captured Baghdad, the demobilization began. The first result was widespread lawlessness, including systematic looting. The Iraqi army had been a respected institution among Iraqis. It had provided law and order. When it was gone, there was nothing to replace it. In addition, thousands of young military men suddenly found that they did not have jobs. Here was another source of discontent available for exploitation by the enemies of the coalition.

Opponents of the U.S. military intervention to topple Saddam Hussein—in Iraq, in the United States, and around the world—have pointed to the ongoing instability and violence in Iraq as evidence that they were correct in their opposition. They argue, in the complete absence of reliable data, that the number of Iraqi civilians who have perished since the war began in 2003 is comparable to the number of innocent Iraqis destroyed by Saddam Hussein.

AN IRAQI ARMY OFFICER *(ON RIGHT, FACING RIGHT)* **SPEAKS WITH MEMBERS** of an anti-al-Qaeda group (in orange jackets) south of Baghdad. U.S. soldiers patrol at left. Many groups battle for control of Iraq, making stability a difficult goal to achieve in the country.

The cost of ending Saddam's dictatorship has indeed been staggering. According to the United Nations High Commissioner for Refugees, more than four million Iraqis have fled their homes or left Iraq altogether. In addition, observers have called into question the ability of Sunnis, Shiites, and Kurds to share power and govern Iraq as a single nation. This, too, remains to be seen.

The nations that lie along the borders of Iraq also have an enormous stake in the future of Iraq. Some, like Iran, hope to gain influence over Iraq, while others, such as Turkey, fear that growing Kurdish self-determination will cause instability on their own soil.

As of early 2008, the struggle to shape Iraq's future continues. What will happen to Iraq after Saddam's fall remains an open question.

WHO'S WHO?

MICHEL AFLAQ (1910–1989): Michel Aflaq was born in Syria to a middle-class Christian family. Disturbed by French control of Syria after World War I, Aflaq was an early proponent of Arab nationalism. He attended university in France, where he came to support Socialism, as well. In 1946 he founded the Baath Party, which supported the formation of a single Arab Socialist state. When Saddam Hussein went into exile after his involvement in a failed assassination attempt, he met Aflaq and, with his assistance, became a full member of the Baath Party. Although the Baath Party came to power in Iraq, it betrayed Aflaq's ideals. Nevertheless, Saddam built him a magnificent tomb in Baghdad following his death from natural causes in 1989.

TARIQ AZIZ (B. 1936): Born to a Chaldean Catholic family, Aziz worked as a journalist and began to rise through the ranks of Iraqi politics. He served as a member of the Regional Command Council—the Baath Party's highest governing unit—from 1974 to 1977, and in 1977 became a member of Saddam's Revolutionary Command Council. In 1979 Aziz was named deputy prime minister of Iraq, where his primary role was to serve as a diplomat explaining Iraq's policies to the world. He later became foreign minister. He surrendered to U.S. forces in April 2003 and remains in custody.

AHMAD HASSAN AL-BAKR (1914–1982): Born in Tikrit, Iraq, Bakr taught school for several years before joining the Iraqi army. An ultranationalist, he took part in the revolt against the British in 1941. He was one of the Free Officers who overthrew the monarchy in 1958. He became prime minister after the 1963 Baathist coup. Driven from office later that year, he regained power in the 1968 Baathist coup. He served as president of Iraq until Saddam Hussein forced him to retire in 1979. His death in 1982 has been attributed to murder by Saddam's agents.

SADDAM HUSSEIN (1937–2006): President of Iraq from 1979, Saddam retained absolute power until his 2003 overthrow by U.S. forces. Born into poverty in a village near Tikrit, Saddam never knew his father. His stepfather kept him out of school and forced him into petty crime to support the family. Saddam emerged from this background tough, crude, and thuggish. In 1955 he moved to Baghdad to attend high school and there became involved with the Baath Party. After taking part in a failed attempt to assassinate Iraq's prime minister, he fled the country. While in exile, Saddam continued his education and acquired a veneer of sophistication. With the fall of Iraq's government, Saddam returned home and married his cousin Sajida. They had two sons and three daughters. U.S. troops captured Saddam in 2003. The new Iraqi government tried him for mass murder. He was found guilty and executed in 2006.

ALI HASSAN AL-MAJID (B. 1941): Saddam Hussein's cousin, born in Tikrit, Iraq, the poor and uneducated al-Majid became one of Saddam's most trusted servants. He served as Iraq's defense minister, interior minister, security chief, bureau secretary of northern Iraqi affairs, military governor of Kuwait, and director of the Revolutionary Command Council. Due to his use of chemical weapons against Kurdish rebels in 1987–1988, he came to be known as Chemical Ali. He was subsequently linked to the suppression of Shiites in southern Iraq. Captured by U.S. forces in August 2003, al-Majid stood trial for mass murder and showed no remorse. On June 24, 2007, an Iraqi court sentenced him to death by hanging.

NEBUCHADNEZZAR II (CA. 630–562 B.C.): The last great leader of Mesopotamia before it fell under foreign domination, Nebuchadnezzar was a brilliant military leader who expanded his empire to encompass Syria. Following this victory, he ascended the throne in 605 B.C. In his repeated military campaigns, recounted in the Bible, he captured Jerusalem and invaded Egypt. Nebuchadnezzar is also known for having restored Babylon to its former splendor by building magnificent temples and creating its famous hanging gardens.

ABDUL KARIM QASIM (1914–1963): A former schoolteacher who became a high-ranking army officer, Qasim led a military coup against the monarchy in 1958. He was rumored to have given the order to shoot the royal family, most of whom died of their wounds. Qasim's rule as prime minister of Iraq was marred by controversy and political conflicts. In 1959 Saddam Hussein participated in a failed attempt to assassinate Qasim. After the Baathist coup of 1963, Qasim was executed.

MUHAMMAD BAKR AL-SADR (1935–1980): The Ayatollah Muhammad Bakr al-Sadr was a prominent Shiite cleric and writer who promoted strict Islamic values. The Baathist government jailed him repeatedly for his views. Sadr founded the opposition Call of Islam Party, which engineered an assassination attempt against two high-ranking government officials. Saddam outlawed the party and ordered the ayatollah and his sister arrested and executed.

AMINA AL-SADR (1938–1980): Amina is the sister of Ayatollah Muhammed Bakr al-Sadr. She was an educator and writer. She founded several religious schools for girls, wrote articles for a religious journal, and organized demonstrations for her brother's freedom. Known as Bint al-Huda (Daughter of the Righteous), she was tortured and executed along with her brother.

KHAIRALLAH TULFAH (?–1992): Saddam's maternal uncle, Khairallah served in the Iraqi army until 1941. An ardent nationalist, and also pro-Nazi, he spent four years in prison for his role in a coup against Iraq's government. Lacking a father, Saddam looked up to his uncle and fell under his political influence. Saddam lived with him in Baghdad and later married Khairallah's daughter, Sajida. Khairallah was appointed mayor of Baghdad by his nephew in 1982. He died of natural causes ten years later.

TIMELINE

2000–1600 B.C. The ancient kingdom of Babylonia flourishes in the Fertile Crescent, the region that extends from the southeast coast of the Mediterranean around the Syrian Desert north of Saudi Arabia to the Persian Gulf.

750–600 B.C. The kingdom of Assyria controls the Fertile Crescent and Mesopotamia, the land between the Tigris and Euphrates rivers. Part of this region becomes modern-day Iraq.

539 B.C. The Persians conquer the Assyrians.

331 B.C. Alexander the Great drives the Persians from Mesopotamia.

A.D. 226 The Sassanid Empire assumes control of Mesopotamia.

762 The caliphs, followers of Muhammad, establish Baghdad, the present-day capital of Iraq, as the center of the Muslim empire on the Arabian Peninsula. The city thrives as a center of culture and learning.

1258 Mongol warriors destroy Baghdad.

1534 The Ottoman Empire establishes Turkish control over Mesopotamia, which is retained until World War I.

1908 Oil deposits are discovered in the Middle East, setting off competition among Western powers for control of the region.

1914 World War I erupts in Europe.

1916 The secret Sykes-Picot Agreement, in anticipation of a Turkish defeat in World War I, divides Mesopotamia between the British and French. Arab nationalists, who had been led to believe that self-government would be their reward for their help in defeating the Turks, believe they have been betrayed.

1920 The victors of World War I grant the British control of three provinces comprising modern Iraq: Mosul, Baghdad, and Basra. The population rises up in revolt against the British, who suppress the revolt within months.

1932 On October 3, Iraq officially becomes an independent nation, a monarchy ruled by King Faisal. However, the British retain a military presence and considerable influence in Iraq.

1936–1968 Numerous coups and changes of government cause more than three decades of instability.

1968 The Baath Party seizes control of Iraq's government for the second time in five years.

1979 In July Saddam Hussein coerces Iraq's President Bakr into resigning and transferring power to him. On July 22, President Saddam Hussein consolidates his power by ousting key members of the RCC on false charges and having them executed.

1980 Iraqi forces invade the Islamic republic of Iran.

1988 The Iran–Iraq War ends with neither side victorious, despite its enormous human and economic cost. Nevertheless, Saddam claims victory.

1990 Iraq invades Kuwait in August and overruns it in a matter of hours. Saddam announces his intention to annex Kuwait and make it Iraq's nineteenth province.

1991 In January a U.S.-led coalition begins Operation Desert Storm, the Gulf War, against Iraq.

In February the coalition ousts Iraqi forces from Kuwait and then suspends hostilities, leaving Saddam in power.

In March Iraqis rebel against Saddam. A fearful international community fails to back the rebels, and Saddam crushes them.

1991–2003 The UN imposes economic sanctions on Iraq and conducts periodic inspections in an attempt to prevent Iraq from producing WMD. These actions succeed only in causing widespread deprivation and suffering among the general population.

2003 On March 19, the Iraq War begins with aerial bombardment by a U.S.-led coalition.

On April 9, Saddam Hussein goes into hiding to evade capture.

On December 13, U.S. troops capture Saddam Hussein, who has been hiding in an underground bunker.

2006 After being convicted in an Iraqi court on charges of mass murder, Saddam Hussein is hanged by Iraqi authorities on December 30.

2007 On January 9, U.S. president George W. Bush announces a "surge," a twenty-thousand increase in the number of U.S. troops to be deployed in Iraq to improve stability and security.

On June 24, Ali Hassan al-Majid, known as Chemical Ali, is sentenced to death for genocide, war crimes, and crimes against humanity.

2008 The U.S. State Department issues a report that the troop surge has resulted in a reduction of violence and a decrease in military and civilian casualties in Baghdad, although the overall situation in Iraq remains volatile.

GLOSSARY

Arab: an Arabic-speaking native of Arabia, a largely desert peninsula of southwestern Asia. Most ancient Arabs were nomadic.

Arabia: an arid peninsula of southwestern Asia that includes the nations of Saudi Arabia, Yemen, Oman, Bahrain, Kuwait, Qatar, and the United Arab Emirates

atheist: a person or political ideology that denies the existence of God

attaché: an official assigned to work at an embassy

Baath: the name of a political party dedicated to revitalizing Arab society by uniting all Arabs into a single state. *Baath* means "resurrection" or "renaissance" in Arabic. It was the ruling party of Iraq, presiding over a one-party dictatorship, from 1968 to 2003.

caliph: a political or spiritual leader of an Islamic state. Traditionally, a caliph is a successor to Muhammad. *Caliph* is derived from the Arabic word for "successor."

clan: an extended family group that, in some societies, serves as the basic unit of social organization

Cold War: the period from 1945 to 1991 during which the United States and the Soviet Union competed for influence over the rest of the world

commissars: political party officials whose job it is to ensure loyalty and obedience to party rules

coup: sudden overthrow of the government; from the French *coup d'état,* or "blow to the state"

cult of personality: a systematic policy of promoting public adoration of a dictator in order to keep that person in power

embargo: a prohibition on trade in specific goods with specific nations that is imposed by governments in wartime

insurgents: people conducting an insurrection, or rebellion, against government authority

League of Nations: an international association founded to prevent future wars and foster peace, established in 1920 after the end of World War I. It was dissolved in 1946 and replaced by the United Nations.

Pan-Arabism: a political philosophy that supports the union of all Arabs into a single Arab nation. Pan-Arabism existed primarily for cooperation in ending Western colonialism in the region.

regent: acting ruler; the person who governs while the hereditary monarch is absent, incapacitated, or too young to rule

Shiite: one of Islam's two major sects, whose followers support Muhammad's son-in-law as his true successor. The name *Shiite* comes from the Arabic word meaning "partisan," or supporter, because of this belief.

Socialism: an economic system in which the community owns all property and operates all businesses with the aim of sharing the work and profits equally

Soviet Union: a former federation of fifteen republics that included Russia, Ukraine, and other nations of eastern Europe and northern Asia

Sunni: one of Islam's two major sects, whose followers believe in electing Muhammad's successors. The name *Sunni* comes from the Arabic word for "tradition" and refers to a supplement to the Quran, Islam's holy book.

welfare state: a system in which the government takes primary responsibility for the individual and social well-being of its citizens

SELECETED BIBLIOGRAPHY

Balaghi, Shiva. *Saddam Hussein: A Biography.* Westport, CT: Greenwood Press, 2006.

Braude, Joseph. *The New Iraq: Rebuilding the Country for Its People, the Middle East, and the World.* New York: Basic Books, 2003.

Coughlin, Con. *Saddam: His Rise and Fall.* New York: Harper Perennial, 2002.

Dodge, Toby. *Inventing Iraq: The Failure of Nation-Building and a History Denied.* New York: Columbia University Press, 2003.

Farouk-Sluglett, Marion, and Peter Sluglett. *Iraq Since 1958: From Revolution to Dictatorship.* London: I. B. Tauris, 2003.

Khalili, Samer al-. *Republic of Fear: The Politics of Modern Iraq.* Berkeley: University of California Press, 1989.

Main, Ernest. *Iraq: From Mandate to Independence.* London: George Allen & Unwin, 1935.

Munthe, Turi, ed. *The Saddam Hussein Reader.* New York: Thunder's Mouth Press, 2002.

Neshat, Saeid N. "A Look into the Woman's Movement in Iraq." *Farzaneh*, 6:11. Spring 2003. http://www.farzanehjournal.com/archive/archive11.htm (May 2007).

Rabil, Robert G. "Oppression by Procedure: The Making of Saddam's Executioners." *Review*, April 2003. http://www.aijac.org.au/review/2003/284/essay284.html (May 2007).

Sasson, Jean P. *Mayada, Daughter of Iraq: One Woman's Survival under Saddam Hussein.* New York: Dutton, 2003.

Sciolino, Elaine. *The Outlaw State: Saddam Hussein's Quest for Power and the Gulf Crisis.* New York: John Wiley & Sons, 1991.

Tripp, Charles. *A History of Iraq.* Cambridge: Cambridge University Press, 2000.

FURTHER READING AND WEBSITES

Anderson, Dale. *Saddam Hussein*. Minneapolis: Twenty-First Century Books, 2004. This biography of one of the world's most notorious dictators covers the life of Saddam Hussein from his childhood in Tikrit to the coalition invasion of Iraq in 2003.

Balaghi, Shiva. *Saddam Hussein: A Biography*. Westport, CT: Greenwood Press, 2006. This brief biography ends with Saddam's capture in 2003.

Khalili, Samer al-. *Republic of Fear: The Politics of Modern Iraq*. Berkeley: University of California Press, 1989. Because this book was written during the height of Saddam's power, the author had to worry about reprisals against himself and his family. Consequently, he neither mentioned the names of his sources nor wrote under his own name. Now living in the United States, the author has republished the book under his own name, Kanan Makiya.

Polk, William R. *Understanding Iraq*. New York: Harper Perennial, 2006. This history of Iraq extends from ancient times through the current American occupation.

Taus-Bolstad, Stacy. *Iraq in Pictures*. Minneapolis: Twenty-First Century Books, 2004. This title, part of the Visual Geography Series®, presents the history and government, economy, people, geography, and culture of Iraq.

Windawi, Thura al-. Translated by Robin Bray. *Thura's Diary: My Life in Wartime Iraq*. New York: Viking, 2004. A nineteen-year-old girl kept this diary, beginning on March 13, 2003, in Baghdad, and ending with the capture of Saddam Hussein in December.

Eden Again: Restoration of the Mesopotamian Marshlands

http://www.edenagain.org/

Eden Again is a project begun in 2001 by Iraqi expatriates. The website describes the effort to reverse the damage done to a unique ecosystem by Saddam's 1990s-era drainage projects.

Human Rights Watch

http://www.hrw.org/

The official website of Human Rights Watch contains reports on the state of human rights throughout the world, including Iraq.

Iraqi Crisis Reports

http://www.iwpr.net/

Published on the Iraq page of the Institute of War and Peace Reporting website, the Iraqi Crisis Reports include firsthand accounts by Iraqis on conditions in Iraq.

Iraq the Model: New Points of View about the Future of Iraq

http://iraqthemodel.blogspot.com/

Two Iraqi brothers post their views on this site. The site also provides numerous links to additional blogs and articles by both Iraqis and Americans.

vgsbooks.com

http://www.vgsbooks.com

Visit vgsbooks.com, the home page of the Visual Geography Series®. You can get linked to all sorts of useful online information, including geographical, historical, demographic, cultural, and economic websites. The vgsbooks.com site is a great resource for late-breaking news.

SOURCE NOTES

7 Elaine Sciolino, *The Outlaw State: Saddam Hussein's Quest for Power and the Gulf Crisis* (New York: John Wiley & Sons, 1991), 89.

8 Con Coughlin, *Saddam: His Rise and Fall* (New York: Harper Perennial, 2002), 158.

8 Said K. Aburish, "How Saddam Hussein Came to Power," in Turi Munthe, ed., *The Saddam Hussein Reader* (New York: Thunder's Mouth Press, 2002), 53.

9 Coughlin, 159.

16 Xenophon, *Anabasis*, quoted in R. Ernest Dupuy and Trevor N. Dupuy, *The Encyclopedia of Military History from 3500 B.C. to the Present* (New York: Harper & Row, 1970), 33.

23 H. V. F. Winstone, *Gertrude Bell* (New York: Quartet Books, 1978), 222.

24 Toby Dodge, *Inventing Iraq: The Failure of Nation-Building and a History Denied* (New York: Columbia University Press, 2003), 29.

32 Coughlin, 7.

36 Shiva Balaghi, *Saddam Hussein: A Biography* (Westport, CT: Greenwood Press, 2006), 27.

36–37 Coughlin, 30.

38 Ibid., 35.

39 Ibid., 41.

39 Balaghi, 33.

42 Samer al-Khalili, *Republic of Fear: The Politics of Modern Iraq* (Berkeley: University of California Press, 1989), 50.

43 Coughlin, 76.

43 al-Khalili, 52.

44 Balaghi, 48.

45 John Bulloch, *The Making of a War: The Middle East from 1967 to 1973* (London: Longman, 1974), 131.

50   Charles Tripp, "The Iran-Iraq War and the Iraqi State," in Turi Munthe, ed., *The Saddam Hussein Reader* (New York: Thunder's Mouth Press, 2002), 109.

56   Coughlin, 181–182.

57   GlobalSecurity.org, "Iran-Iraq War (1980–1988)," *GlobalSecurity.org*, April 27, 2005, http://www .globalsecurity.org/ military/world/war/iran -iraq.htm (May 2007).

59–60   U.S. Department of State, "Saddam's Chemical Weapons Campaign: Halabja, March 16, 1988," *U.S. Department of State*, March 14, 2003, http:// www.state.gov/r/pa/ei/ rls/18714.htm (May 2007).

62   Coughlin, 234.

68   Franklin Foer, "How Saddam Manipulates the U.S. Media Air War," *New Republic*, October 16, 2002, http://www.tnr.com/doc. mhtml?i=20021028&s =foer102802&c=2 (May 2007).

70   Margaret Thatcher, *The Downing Street Years* (New York: HarperCollins, 1993), 817.

70–71   The Middle East Research Institute of Japan, "Iraqi Revolutionary Command Council Statement on Merger with Kuwait, 8 August 1990," http://www. meij.or.jp/text/Gulf%20 War/rccstat.htm (May 2007).

71   GlobalSecurity.org, "Allied Troop Contributions," *GlobalSecurity.org*, April 27, 2005, http://www .globalsecurity.org/ military/ops/desert _stormallied.htm (May 2007).

75   Thomas W. Kelly, *Arlington National Cemetery Website*, December 24, 2006, http:// www.arlingtoncemetery.net/ twkelly.htm, (June 2007).

75   Zainab al-Suwaij, "The Fire Last Time," *New Republic*, February 3, 2003, http:// www.tnr.com/doc .mhtml?i=20030210&s =alsuwaij021003 (May 2007).

77   Coughlin, 281.

77–78   Human Rights Watch, "The Iraqi Government Assault on the Marsh Arabs," *hrw.org*, January 2003, http://www.hrw.org/backgrounder/mena/marsharabs1.htm (May 2007).

78   Sciolino, 95.

78   Ibid.

79–80   Human Rights Watch, "Endless Torment: The 1991 Uprising in Iraq and Its Aftermath," *hrw.org*, June 1992, 1, http://www.hrw.org/reports/1992/Iraq926.htm (May 2007).

84–85   Jean P. Sasson, *Mayada, Daughter of Iraq: One Woman's Survival under Saddam Hussein* (New York: Dutton, 2003), 104.

87   Ofra Bengio, "Saddam's Word," in Turi Munthe, ed., *The Saddam Hussein Reader* (New York: Thunder's Mouth Press, 2002), 80.

87   Sciolino, 51.

87   Bengio, 84.

88   Marion Farouk-Sluglett and Peter Sluglett, *Iraq Since 1958: From Revolution to Dictatorship* (London: I. B. Tauris, 2003), 262.

89–90   Ibid., 253.

91   Efraim Karsh and Lawrence Freedman, "Saddam Hussein and the Gulf War," in Turi Munthe, ed., *The Saddam Hussein Reader* (New York: Thunder's Mouth Press, 2002), 223.

94   Sciolino, 82.

96   al-Khalili, 74.

97   Robert G. Rabil, "Oppression by Procedure: The Making of Saddam's Executioners," *Review*, April 2003, http://www.aijac.org.au/review/2003/284/essay284.html (May 2007).

98   Sciolino, 11.

98   Human Rights Watch, "The Institutions of Repression," in Turi Munthe, ed., *The Saddam Hussein Reader* (New York: Thunder's Mouth Press, 2002), 179.

99   al-Khalili, 67.

99   Amnesty International
     USA, "Annual Report on
     Iraq 1978," 259, *Amnesty
     International USA*, 2007,
     http://www.amnestyusa
     .org/Iraq/Past_Annual
     _Reports_on_Iraq/page
     .do?id=1101892&n1
     =30&n2=30&n3=923
     (May 2007).

99   Sasson, 55.

99   Amnesty Internationa
     USA, "Annual Report on
     Iraq 1985," 314, *Amnesty
     International USA*, 2007,
     http://www.amnestyusa
     .org/Iraq/Past
     _AnnualReports_on_Iraq/
     page.do?id=1101892&n1
     =30&n2=30&n3=923
     (May 2007).

100 Ann Clwyd, "Iraq Is
     Free at Last," *Guardian
     Unlimited*, March 30,
     2004, http://www
     .guardian.co.uk/Iraq/
     Story/0,2763,1180843,00
     .html (June 2004).

100 Sasson, 71.

101 Coughlin, 171.

101 The White House,
     "Saddam Hussein's
     Repression of the Iraqi
     People," *The White
     House, President George
     W. Bush, Policies in
     Focus*, September 2002,
     http://www.whitehouse
     .gov/infocus/iraq/
     decade/sect4.html (May
     2007).

102 CIA, "The World
     Factbook 2007," *Central
     Intelligence Agency*,
     2007, https://www.cia
     .gov/cia/publications/
     factbook/geos/iz (May
     2007).

108 Sasson, 134.

108 Sciolino, 67.

110 Sasson, 155–160.

110 Ibid.

110 Ibid.

111 Ibid.

112 Human Rights Watch,
     "The Institutions of
     Repression," 183.

112 Sciolino, 116.

112–113 Joseph Braude, *The New*

Iraq: Rebuilding the Country for Its People, the Middle East, and the World (New York: Basic Books, 2003), 87.

116 Ibid., 117.

116 Ibid.

117 Ibid., 115.

119 Balaghi, 53.

120 Braude, 20.

120 Ibid., 170.

121 Human Rights Watch, "The Institutions of Repression," 176.

121 Saeid N. Neshat, "A Look into the Woman's Movement in Iraq," *Farzaneh*, 6:11, 56, Spring 2003, http://www .farzanehjournal.com/ archive (May 2007).

123 Ibid., 58–59.

126 Mark Bowden, "Tales of the Tyrant," *Atlantic Monthly*, May 2002, http:// www.theatlantic.com/ doc/200205/bowden (May 2007).

127 UN, "Security Council Resolution 1441 (2002): The Situation between Iraq and Kuwait," *United Nations*, 2007, http:// www.un.org/Docs/ scres/2002/sc2002 .htm (June 2007).

128 Coughlin, 330.

129–130 The White House, "President Says Saddam Hussein Must Leave Iraq within 48 Hours," *The White House*, March 17, 2003, http://www .whitehouse.gov/news/ releases/2003/03/ 200303177.html (June 2007).

131 Balaghi, 150.

133 Coughlin, 368.

133 Ibid.

134 Library of Congress, "Trial of Saddam Hussein," *The Law Library of Congress*, June 20, 2006, http:// www.loc.gov/law/public/ saddam/saddam_back .html (June 2007).

134 Coughlin, 378.

INDEX

PHOTO ACKNOWLEDGMENTS

The images in this book are used with the permission of: © Thomas Hartwell/Time & Life Pictures/Getty Images, p. 1; © AFP/Getty Images, pp. 7, 29, 38; © Karim Sahib/AFP/Getty Images, pp. 9, 106; © Laura Westlund/Independent Picture Service, pp. 11, 79; © Oleg Nikishin/Getty Images, p. 13; © Visual Arts Library (London)/Alamy, p. 18; Library of Congress, pp. 21 (LC-DIG-ggbain-20814), 22 (LC-DIG-matpc-13163); © Folb/Topical Press Agency/Hulton Archive/Getty Images, p. 27 (left); AP Photo/Str, p. 27 (right); © Popperfoto/Getty Images, p. 31; © Getty Images, p. 39; AP Photo, pp. 43, 49; © Keystone/Getty Images, p. 51; AP Photo/Zuheir Saade, p. 52; AP Photo/Greg English, pp. 60, 71; © John Kreul/Independent Picture Service, p. 63; © Ahmad Al-Rubaye/AFP/Getty Images, p. 65; AP Photo/Denis Paquin, p. 80; © REUTERS/Damir Sagolj, p. 88; AP Photo/INA, p. 93; AP Photo/Jerome Delay, p. 95; © Laurent van Der Stock/Gamma/Eyedea/ZUMA Press, p. 115; AP Photo/Jassim Mohammed, pp. 117, 127; © Scott Peterson/Getty Images, p. 118; © Francoise De Mulder/Roger Viollet/Getty Images, p. 122; © Kurt Vinion/Getty Images, p. 129; © John Li/Getty Images, p. 130; AP Photo/Nikola Solic, Pool, p. 135; © Mauricio Lima/AFP/Getty Images, p. 139.

Cover: AP Photo/Hussein Malla (main); © Bill Hauser/Independent Picture Service (background).

AUTHOR BIOGRAPHY

James R. Arnold was born in Illinois, and his family moved to Switzerland when he was a teenager. Arnold has written more than twenty books about American and European history and contributed to many others. He and his wife, Roberta Wiener, live and farm in Virginia.